Keto Diet For Beginners 2019

The Detailed Ketogenic Diet Guide

For Losing Weight, Transform Your Body And Living The Keto Lifestyle

With A 30-Day Meal Plan

(Bonus Recipes And Meal Preps Included)

Table of Contents

Introduction..1

Chapter 1: The Keto Diet & How It Works 3

Chapter 2: Ketogenic Foods & Supplements.........................19

Chapter 3: Keto Breakfast Options....................................... 27

Chapter 4: Keto Lunch: Salads - Soups & Pasta.................... 62

Chapter 5: Keto Dinner Favorites: Fish & Poultry 96

Chapter 6: Keto Dinner Options: Pork & Other Meat Favorites
.... 120

Chapter 7: Keto Appetizers: Side Dishes & Bread.................135

Chapter 8: Keto Desserts & Smoothies 166

Chapter 9: 30-Day Ketogenic Meal Plan 191

A Final Word: Tips & Tricks For Success 206

Index 211

Introduction

Congratulations on purchasing the *Keto Diet For Beginners 2019,* and thank you for doing so. I have filled it with tons of recipes to suit your desires for breakfast, lunch, dinner, and desserts. Everyone will surely find a new favorite!

Your new meal plan will provide you with many new ways to change your lifestyle. You will never be hungry and will still remain within the constraints of the keto plan. Before we begin the journey, let's discover how the plan was originated.

The Ketogenic methods date back in time. During the progression of history, as early as the 20th century, fasting was theorized by Bernard McFadden, otherwise known as Bernarr Macfadden, as a means for restoring your health. One of his students introduced a treatment for epilepsy using the same plan. In 1912, it was reported by the *New York Medical Journal* that fasting is a successful method to treat epileptic patients, followed by a starch-free and sugar-free diet.

By 1921, Rollin Woodyatt, an endocrinologist noted the liver produced the ketone bodies (three water-soluble compounds); acetone, β-hydroxybutyrate, and acetoacetate) as a result of a diet highly rich in fats and consisting of low amounts of carbohydrates at the same time.

Also, in 1921, Dr. Russell Wilder who worked for the Mayo Clinic became well-known when he formulated the ketogenic format which was then used as part of the epilepsy therapy treatment plan. He had a massive interest in the program because he also suffered from epilepsy. The ketogenic methods also became known for its assistance with weight loss and many other ailments.

By following the guidelines provided, you will begin the process of putting your body into a state called ketosis. It sounds complicated, but it's a natural healing process. Your body will adapt to burning the ketones instead of glucose. Fruits, starches, sugar, grains and other foods contain sugar/glucose. When your body has zero glucose, it will burn fat stored in your body.

Chapter 1: The Keto Diet & How It Works

In many cases, you are currently burning glucose as your 'fuel' source which in turn will change your food into energy. The remainder of the glucose develops into fat and is stored in your body to be consumed at a later time.

The keto diet will set up your body to deplete the stored glucose. Once that is accomplished, your body will focus on diminishing the stored fat you have saved as fuel. Many people don't understand that counting calories don't matter at this point since it is just used as a baseline.

Your body doesn't need glucose which will trigger these two stages:

- *The State of Glycogenesis*: The excess of glucose converts itself into glycogen which is stored in the muscles and liver. Research indicates only about half of your energy used daily can be saved as glycogen.

- *The State of Lipogenesis:* This phase is introduced when there is an adequate supply of glycogen in your liver and muscles, with any excess being converted to fat and stored.

Your body will have no more food (much like when you are sleeping) making your body burn the fat to create ketones. Once the ketones break down the fats, which generate fatty acids, they will burn-off in the liver through beta-oxidation. Thus, when you no longer have a supply of glycogen or glucose, ketosis begins and will use the consumed/stored fat as energy.

The Internet provides you with several ways to calculate your daily intake of carbs. Try a <u>keto calculator</u> to assist you. Begin your weight loss process by making a habit of checking your levels when you want to know what essentials your body needs during the course of your dieting plan. You will document your personal information such as height and weight. The Internet calculator will provide you with essential math.

When the glycerol and fatty acid molecules are released, the ketogenesis process begins, and acetoacetate is produced. The Acetoacetate is converted to two types of ketone units:

- *Acetone:* This is mostly excreted as waste but can also be metabolized into glucose. This is the reason individuals on a ketogenic diet will experience a distinctive smelly breath.

- *Beta-hydroxybutyrate or BHB:* Your muscles will convert the acetoacetate into BHB which will fuel your brain after you have been on the keto diet for a short time.

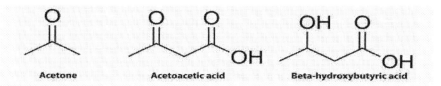

Acetone   Acetoacetic acid   Beta-hydroxybutyric acid

You will discover how flexible the ketogenic methods are when coupled with the intermittent fasting techniques. Each will lose weight differently, and other people may not have the same goals as you.

For now, as a beginner, you will begin by using the first method as shown below. This is an important step; you must decide how you want to proceed with your diet plan. It is always best to discuss this essential step with your physician. These are the four methods, so you better understand the different levels of the keto diet plan:

Keto Method # 1: The standard ketogenic diet (SKD) consists of moderate protein, high-fat, and is low in carbs. Generally, this diet is considered a low-carbohydrate (5% average), high-fat (75% average), and moderate protein (20%) diet plan. These are average counts and can vary.

Keto Method # 2: Workout times will call for the targeted keto diet, which is also called TKD. The process consists of adding additional carbohydrates to the diet plan during the times when you are more active. This is popular with sportsmen and women who are much more active.

Keto Method # 3: The cyclical ketogenic diet (CKD) entails a restricted five-day keto diet plan followed by two high-carbohydrate days.

Keto Method 4: The high-protein keto diet is comparable to the standard keto plan (SKD) in all aspects. You will consume more protein. Its ratio is repeatedly noted as maintaining 35% protein, 5% carbs, and 60% fat. (Once again, these are average percentages.)

How to Begin:

Step 1: Choose a non-stressful week to begin the ketogenic diet plan.

Step 2: Purge the pantry and fridge.

Step 3: Restock the fridge and pantry with ketogenic food items.

Step 4: Consider skipping one meal each day. Maybe sleep a little longer and have brunch.

Step 5: Initially, don't exceed your net carbs and don't limit the fat and protein you consume.

Step 6: Make a routine. Drink a large glass of water and have a supplement of a ½ teaspoon of MCT oil or 2 teaspoons of coconut oil.

Step 7: Keep track of your ketone levels.

Macros & How To Calculate For Ketosis

The first step is understanding the macronutrients and how they're calculated.

The macronutrients are building blocks of food consisting of protein, fat, and carbs. You will need to try one of the apps discussed later to discover what your 'keto numbers' are for daily consumption since each individual has a different amount allowed because of specific elements.

Maintain your weight with a balance of high fats and low carbs. To achieve weight loss, you will need to reduce your carbohydrate intake. The ketogenic techniques will provide you with the required foods to lose weight and not be hungry. Macros are found in varying amounts which are measured using grams. For example, fat equals approximately 9 calories per gram, protein at 4 calories, and the carbs at 4 calories for each gram.

Count The Calories Or The Micros: Which Is Best?

The short of counting calories is that they don't tell the whole story. You can fill up on the 'right' calories, and you may also lose muscle mass. For example, you count one hundred calories of avocado (a fat) which is better than a one hundred calorie cookie (carbs). That is why keto counts the macros (fat, protein, and carbs) not the calories.

Remember This Formula: You will need to calculate your net carbs on some of the recipes you discover on the Internet — some list only the total carbs. If that happens, just take the total carbs listed (-) fiber (=) the total net carbs which is what you need to track for an accurate count so you can remain in ketosis.

Guidelines For The Ketogenic Way Of Living

Ketogenic 0-20 Carbs Daily: Generally this low level of carbs is related to a restrictive medical diet whereby the patient is restricted from 10 to 15 grams each day to ensure the proper levels of ketosis remains. The Charlie Foundation is one of the plans used to promote the treatment of epilepsy.

Moderate 20-50 Daily Carbs Allowed: If you have diabetes, are obese, or metabolically deranged, this is the plan for you. If you are consuming less than the 50 grams daily; your body will achieve a ketosis state which supplies the ketone bodies.

Liberal 50-100 Daily Carbs Allowed: This option is best if you're active and lean and are attempting to maintain your weight.

Symptoms Of Ketosis

- *Keto Flu/Induction Flu:* The diet can make you irritable, nauseous, a bit confused, lethargic, and you may also suffer from a lingering headache. Several days into the plan should remedy these effects. Just in case it doesn't, add one-half of a teaspoon of salt to a glass of water, and drink it to help with the side effects. You may need to do this once a day for about the first week, and it could take about 15 to 20 minutes before it helps. Relax, it will go away soon!

- *Digestive Issues:* You have made an enormous change in your diet overnight. It's expected that you may have problems including constipation or diarrhea when you first start the keto diet. This is yet another reason why you must drink plenty of water. The low-carbs contribute to the digestive issues. Each person is different, and it will depend on your chosen diet plan and what foods you have chosen to eat to increase your fiber intake. Try not to introduce new foods into your daily meal regimen until the transitional phase of ketosis is concluded. Digestive issues will improve with time.

You may also be lacking beneficial bacteria. Add fermented foods to your diet plan and increase your probiotics to aid digestion issues. You can benefit from the B vitamins, omega 3 fatty acids, and other beneficial enzymes as well. Eat the right veggies and add a small amount of salt to your food to help with the movements. If all else fails, try a dose of *Milk of Magnesia*.

- *Thirst is Increased:* Fluid retention is increased when you are consuming carbohydrates. Keep in mind, that once you have flushed away the carbs, your water weight is lost. You counter-balance by increasing your water intake since you are possibly dehydrated. The ketogenic diet requires more water, since as a result; you are storing carbs. If you are dehydrated; your body can use the stored carbs to restore hydration. When you're in ketosis, the carbs are removed, and your body doesn't have the water reserves.

- *Ketosis and Your Sleep Patterns:* After you have a good night of sleep, your body is in ketosis (since you have fasted for over eight hours); you're well on the way to burning ketones. If you are new to the ketogenic plan (high-fat and low-carb dieting), the optimal fat-burning state takes time. Your body has depended on bringing in carbs and glucose; it will not readily give up carbs and start to crave saturated fats. A restless night is also a typical side effect.

Vitamin supplements can sometimes remedy the problem that can be caused by a lowered insulin and serotonin level. For a quick fix; try one-half of a tablespoon of fruit spread and a square of chocolate. It sounds crazy, but it works! Unfortunately, you still need to count the carbs of your homemade remedy.

- *Leg Cramps*: The loss of magnesium (a mineral) can be a factor that creates pain with the onset of the keto diet plan changes. With the loss of the minerals during urination, you could experience attacks of cramps in your legs.

- *Heart Palpitations*: You may begin to feel 'fluttery' as a result of dehydration or because of an insufficient intake of salt. Try to adjust your menu plan by trying more carbs. If you don't feel better quickly, you should seek emergency care.

In Essence: The Effects of Overconsumption of Carbs In The Body can be <u>lethal to </u>your heart, kidney, and digestive system!

Who Can & Cannot Use The Ketogenic Techniques:

Always, Check Your Medications For Compatibility:

It's important to inform your doctor about your weight loss program. He/she may prescribe some medicines that make you gain weight.

If you are taking insulin injections in high doses, your insulin can impede weight loss. By consuming fewer carbs, you are substantially reducing the requirement of insulin. Again, ask your healthcare professional before you make any changes.

If You Are Attempting To Lose Weight: Be Aware Of Other Probable Medications Causing Weight Gain:

- Oral contraceptives
- Antidepressants
- Epilepsy drugs
- Blood pressure medications
- Allergy medicines
- Antibiotics

If you enjoy working out for your health, be sure to do that at least four hours before sleeping. Make sure your room has sufficient darkness. You will wake refreshed, ready to face your tasty ketogenic breakfast.

Do you take high blood pressure medications? It's not your best move to begin a low-carb diet, including one like keto if you're currently taking other types of blood-pressure medications. If you feel weak, tired, or dizzy; you should check your blood pressure. If it's below 120/80; you should contact your physician to discuss a plan that's workable for you.

Do you breastfeed? You shouldn't participate in a low-carbohydrate diet plan such as the ketogenic method. It's recommended to consume a minimum of 50 grams of carbs daily while breastfeeding. You can choose any way you like to get the extra carbs by selecting moderate and liberal low-carb recipes. Enjoy three fruits daily to boost your diet.

Benefits of The Ketogenic Diet

- *Mental Focus:* Your brain is approximately <u>60% fat</u> by weight. By increasing your fatty foods intake; you will have better focus. It can maintain itself and work at full capacity.

- *Polycystic Ovary Syndrome (PCOS):* Young women of childbearing years can be affected by this disorder. It is further also associated with obesity, insulin resistance, and hyperinsulinemia. One study concluded a significant improvement in weight loss in fasting women over a 24-week period. The group limited carb intake to <u>20 grams </u>daily for the 24 weeks.

- *Dravet Syndrome:* Dravet Syndrome is a severe form of epilepsy which is marked by prolonged, uncontrollable, and frequent seizures which began in infancy. Medications that are available don't improve symptoms and approximately one-third of the Dravet Syndrome patients.

A clinical study used <u>13 children </u>with Dravet Syndrome to stay on the ketogenic diet for more than one year to remain seizure-free. Over 50% of the group decreased in the frequency of the seizures. It was reported that six of the patients stopped the diet later, and one remains seizure-free.

A Special Note For Women: Somewhere along the path, women began to believe that fat was bad and caused weight gain. You now realize this is a myth! You are gaining new methods to improve your health and so much more using the low carb and high-fat techniques combined in keto. Just recall, these are some of your unique advantages using the ketogenic methods if you have any of these symptoms:

- You want to increase your workout performance in the gym
- Have adrenal fatigue
- Feel tired or unmotivated
- Have PCOS
- Have terrible PMS
- Have irregular or absent periods
- Have imbalanced thyroid hormones
- Cannot lose or gain weight no matter what you try
- Get hungry and need to always have a snack handy in between meals
- Have an autoimmune disease you would like to manage

How The Keto Diet Impacts Sports For Men & Women

High-fat diets and low-carb diets may help endurance athletes perform better, but the "team and sprint athletes may see a drop in their performance. Many endurance athletes also turn to Keto diets for losing weight to boost his/her performance.

However, athletes involved in short-duration, high-intensity sports might see drops in performance while using the keto diet plan. The research was provided using sixteen women and men at a St. Louis University by testing the anaerobic exercise performance following either a low-carbohydrate keto diet or a high-carb diet for four days.

Edward Weiss, Ph. D, associate professor of nutrition and dietetics at Saint Louis University, said that the results could make a big difference to athletes involved in sports that depend on short-burst anaerobic activities.

People on the ketogenic diet performed more poorly at anaerobic exercise tasks than those eating more carbs. Depending on the task, their performance was 4 to 15% lower than the high-carbohydrate group.

Weiss added that the study "probably also applies to many aerobic activities, as other studies have demonstrated that high-intensity aerobic exercise performance may be compromised by low-carb diets — including keto."

In light of these results, he advised athletes to avoid these diets unless they have "compelling reasons for following a low-carb diet." Additional studies will provide more insight into the advantages and disadvantages of ketogenic diets for athletic performance. For now, he suggests that athletes "err on the cautious side."

Common Testing Methods Used For Ketosis Monitoring

Maintaining ketosis is an individual process, and you need to be sure you are achieving your goals. The levels of beta-hydroxybutyrate, acetone, and acetoacetate can be measured in your urine, breath, and blood.

You can use a *'Ketonix'* meter to measure your breath. You breathe into the meter. The results will be provided by a special coded color that will flash to show your levels of ketosis at that time.

Measure the ketones with a blood ketone meter. All it takes is a small drop of blood on a testing strip inserted into the meter. This process has been researched as an excellent indicator of your current ketosis levels. Unfortunately, the testing strips are expensive.

Test your urine for acetoacetate. The strip is dipped into the urine which will change the color of the strip. The various shades of purple and pink indicate the levels of the ketones. The darker the color on the testing strip; the higher the level of ketones. The major benefit is they are inexpensive. The most effective time to test is early in the morning after a ketogenic diet dinner the evening before testing.

You should use one or more of these methods to indicate whether you need to adjust your intake of foods to remain in ketosis.

If or when you fast, the hormones in your body will change. The keto plan is similar to this process. You could achieve ketosis in just a couple of days once you have used up all of your stored glycogen. It can take a month or just a few days. It all depends on which type of plan you choose (discussed later). Your protein and carbohydrate intake will determine the time.

Chapter 2: Ketogenic Foods & Supplements

Foods To Eat

Choose Healthy Fats & Oils

Coconut Oil: You vamp up the fat intake with this high flash-point oil. Enjoy a coconut oil smoothie before your workouts. Use it with your meats, chicken, fish or on top of veggies. It will quickly transfer from solid form to oil according to its temperature.

Extra-Virgin Olive Oil (EVOO): Olive oil dates back for centuries – back to where oil was used for anointing kings and priests. High-quality oil with its low-acidity makes the oil have a smoke point as high as 410° Fahrenheit. That's higher than most cooking applications call for, making olive oil more heat-stable than many other cooking fats. It contains (2 tsp.) -0- carbs.

Monounsaturated fats, such as the ones in olive oil, are also linked with better blood sugar regulation, including lower fasting glucose, as well as reducing inflammation throughout the body. Olive oil also helps to prevent cardiovascular disease by protecting the integrity of your vascular system and lowering LDL which is also called the 'bad' cholesterol.

Keto-Friendly Monounsaturated & Saturated Fats:

Include these items (listed in grams):

- Olives – 3 jumbo - 5 large or 10 small – 1 net carb
- Chicken fat/Duck Fat/Beef Tallow – 1 tbsp. 0- net carbs
- Unsweetened flaked coconut – 3 tbsp. – 2 net carbs
- Unsalted Butter/Ghee – 1 tbsp. -0 net carbs
- Egg yolks – 1 large – 0.6 net carbs
- Organic Red Palm oil – ex. Nutiva - 1 tbsp. -0- net carbs

- Avocado oil/Sesame oil – 1 tbsp. -0 net carbs
- Flaxseed oil – 1 tbsp. – 0 net carbs
- Various Dressings
- Keto-Friendly Mayonnaise

Keto-Friendly Sweeteners

Stevia Drops offer delicious flavors including hazelnut, vanilla, English toffee, and chocolate. Some individuals think the drops are too bitter, so at first, use only three drops to equal one teaspoon of sugar.

Xylitol is at the top of the sugary list as an excellent choice to sweeten your teriyaki and barbecue sauce and teriyaki. Its natural-occurring sugar alcohol has a Glycemic index (GI) standing of 13.

Swerve Granular Sweetener is also an excellent choice as a blend. It's made from non-digestible carbs sourced from starchy root veggies and select fruits. Start with 3/4 of a teaspoon for every one of sugar. Increase the portion to your taste.

Foods to Limit

Grains to Avoid:

First, you need to realize grains are made from carbohydrates. This list is based on one cup servings. Avoid bread, pasta, pizza crusts, or crackers and cookies made with these grains:

- Buckwheat: 33 carbs - 6 protein - 1 grams fat
- Wheat: (1 slice wheat bread) 14 carbs - 3 protein - 1 gram fat
- Barley: 44 carbs - 4 protein - 1 gram fat
- Quinoa: 39 carbs - 8 protein - 4 grams fat
- Corn: 32 carbs - 4 protein - 1 grams fat
- Millet: 41 carbs - 6 protein - 2 grams fat
- Bulgur: 33 carbs - 5.6 protein - 0.4 grams fat
- Amaranth: 46 carbs - 9 protein - 4 grams fat
- Oats: 36 carbs - 6 protein - 3 grams fat
- Rice: 45 carbs - 5 protein - 2 grams fat
- Rye: 15 carbs - 3 protein - 1 gram fat

Sugars to Avoid:

- Raw Sugar: 12 grams of carbs - 0 protein - 0 grams fat
- Agave Nectar: 14 grams of carbs - 0 protein - 0 grams fat

- Honey: 17 grams of carbs - 0 protein -0 grams fat
- Maple Syrup: 14 grams of carbs - 0 protein - 0 grams fat
- Cane Sugar: 12 grams of carbs - 0 protein - 0 grams fat
- High-fructose Corn Syrup: 14 grams of carbs - 0 protein -0 grams fat
- Turbinado Sugar: 12 carbs - 0 protein - 0 grams fat

Beans & Legumes To Avoid:

- Kidney Beans: 18.5 carbs - 7 protein - 0.75 grams fat
- Black Beans: 23 carbs -7 protein - 0.5 grams fat
- Chickpeas: 20 carbs - 6 protein - 2 grams fat
- Lentils: 19 carbs - 8 protein - 0 grams fat
- White Beans/Great Northern: 22 carbs - 8 protein - 0 grams fat
- Green Peas: 14 carbs - 4 protein - 0 grams fat
- Lima Beans: carbs - protein - grams fat
- Cannellini Beans: carbs - protein - grams fat
- Black Eyed Peas: 14 carbs - 2 protein - 0 grams fat
- Fava Beans: 17 carbs - 2 protein - 0 grams fat

Starchy Vegetables To Avoid:

- Yams: 19 carbs - 1 protein -0 grams fat

- Sweet Potatoes: 14 carbs - 1 protein - 0 grams fat
- Potatoes (1 medium baked) 28 carbs - 3 protein - 0.3 grams fat
- Carrots: 6 carbs - 1 protein - 0 grams fat
- Corn: 32 carbs - 4 protein - 1 gram fat
- Peas: 14 carbs - 4 protein - 0 grams fat
- Yucca (.5 cup raw) 39 carbs - 1.5 protein - 0 grams fat

Fruits To Avoid:

- Apples – no skin - boiled – 13.6 total carbs
- Apricots - 7.5 total carbs
- Bananas - 23.4 total carbs
- Fresh Blackberries - 5.4 net carbs
- Fresh Blueberries - 8.2 net carbs
- Fresh Strawberries - 3 net carbs
- Cantaloupe - 6 total carbs
- Raw Cranberries - 4 net carbs
- Gooseberries - 8.8 net carbs
- Kiwi – 14.2 total carbs
- Fresh Boysenberries - 8.8 net carbs
- Oranges – 11.7 total carbs
- Peaches - 11.6 total carbs
- Pears – 19.2 total carbs
- Pineapple - 11 total carbs
- Plums – 16.3 total carbs

- Watermelon -7.1 total carbs

Processed Foods:

Don't purchase any items if you see carrageenan on the label. Generally, look for labels with the least amount of ingredients. Usually, the ones that provide the most nutrition are listed in those shorter lists. These are just a few examples of processed snacks to avoid while on a ketogenic diet.:

- Cereal Bars
- Rice cakes
- Flavored Nuts
- Popcorn
- Potato Chips
- Pretzels
- Protein Bars
- Crackers

Keep in mind, these are just guidelines for you to better understand the process of how to use your carbohydrates wisely. For example, you would not want to grab half of a watermelon for a snack (shameless).

Supplements Used On The Ketogenic Plan

You may experience some headaches, fatigue, or nausea which is sometimes called 'induction flu.' As you remove the carbs, your potassium and sodium (key electrolytes) are also removed. Taking a supplement will help with these issues.

Sodium Supplements: You should receive at least one to two grams of extra sodium daily. Some of the pros accomplish this with bouillon cubes. Sea Salt is a great option used in your diet plan. You should receive <u>3000 to 5000</u> mg of sodium daily.

Potassium Supplement: It's possible for you to become low in potassium in the short-term because of the vomiting and diarrhea that could go along with your early stages to the keto plan. Natural potassium can also be received through milk, whole grains, bananas, veggies, peas, and beans. It is recommended to take supplements because potassium also leaves your body with salt. As part of your well-prepared meal plan, you should receive <u>3000 to 4000</u> mg of potassium daily.

Magnesium Supplement: For magnesium, <u>300-500 mg</u> is an initial recommendation. Muscle cramps are your best indicator of depletion.

Chapter 3: Keto Breakfast Options

Bacon Hash

Yields Provided: 2

Nutritional Facts Per Serving:

- 9 g Net Carbs
- 23 g Protein
- 24 g Total Fats
- 366 Calories

Ingredients Needed:
- Small green pepper (1)
- Jalapenos (2)
- Small onion (1)
- Eggs (4)
- Bacon slices (6)

Preparation Steps:
1. Chop the bacon into chunks using a food processor. Set aside for now.
2. Slice the peppers and onions into thin strips and dice the jalapenos as small as possible.
3. Warm up a skillet and fry the veggies.
4. Once browned, combine the fixings and cook until crispy. Place on a serving dish with the eggs.

Blueberry Pancake Bites

Yields Provided: 24 bites

Nutritional Facts Per Serving:
- 7.5 g Net Carbs
- 13 g Total Fats
- 6 g Protein
- 188 Calories

Ingredients Needed:

- Baking powder (1 tsp.)
- Water (.33 - .5 cup)
- Melted ghee (.25 cup)
- Coconut flour (.5 cup)
- Cinnamon (.5 tsp.)
- Salt (.5 tsp.)
- Eggs (4)
- Vanilla extract (.5 tsp.)
- Frozen blueberries (.5 cup)
- *Also Needed*: Muffin tray

Preparation Steps:

1. Warm up the oven to reach 325° Fahrenheit.
2. Use a spritz of coconut oil spray to grease 24 muffin cups.
3. Combine the eggs, sweetener, and vanilla; mixing until smooth. Fold in the flour, melted ghee, salt, baking powder, and cinnamon. Stir in .33 cup of water to finish the batter.
4. The mixture should be thick. Next, divide the batter into the prepared cups with several berries in each one.
5. Bake until set (20-25 min.). Cool.

Brunch Brownies

Yields Provided: 6

Nutritional Facts Per Serving:

- 4 g Net Carbs
- 7 g Protein
- 14 g Total Fats
- 193 Calories

Ingredients Needed:

- Cocoa powder (.25 cup)
- Golden flaxseed meal (1 cup)
- Cinnamon (1 tbsp.)
- Baking powder (.5 tbsp.)
- Salt (.5 tsp.)
- Egg (1 large)
- Coconut oil (2 tbsp.)
- Caramel syrup - Sugar-free (.25 cup)
- Apple cider vinegar (1 tsp.)
- Pumpkin puree (.5 cup)
- Vanilla extract (1 tsp.)
- Slivered almonds (.25 cup)
- *Also Needed*: Muffin tin with 6 paper liners

Preparation Steps:

1. Warm up the oven to 350° Fahrenheit.

2. Line the muffin pan. Mix each of the fixings until well combined.

3. Spoon about ¼ of a cup of the batter into each cup.

4. Sprinkle the almonds over the top of each muffin and press gently.

5. Bake for about 15 minutes.

Choco Breakfast Waffles

Yields Provided: 5

Nutritional Facts Per Serving:
- 3.4 g Net Carbs
- 7 g Protein
- 27 g Total Fats
- 289 Calories

Ingredients Needed:
- Separated eggs (5)
- Unsweetened cocoa (.25 cup)
- Granular sweetener (3 tbsp.)
- Coconut flour (4 tbsp.)
- Baking powder (1 tsp.)
- Melted butter (4.5 oz.)
- Milk of choice (3 tbsp.)
- Vanilla (1 tsp.)

Preparation Steps:

1. Break the eggs into a mixing bowl and whisk the egg whites briskly to form stiff peaks.
2. In another container, whisk the sweetener, baking powder, cocoa, with the egg yolks.
3. Slowly, add the butter to the dry mixture. Stir in the vanilla and milk.
4. Fold in the prepared egg whites a little at a time.
5. Transfer the mixture in the waffle maker and cook until they are golden brown.

Coconut & Walnut Porridge

Yields Provided: 1

Nutritional Facts Per Serving:

- 6 g Net Carbs
- 12 g Protein
- 65 g Total Fats
- 544 Calories

Ingredients Needed:

- Almond butter (1 tbsp.)
- Coconut milk (.5 cup)
- Crushed walnuts (3 tbsp.)
- Desiccated coconut (1.5 tbsp.)
- Coconut oil (1 tbsp.)

- Cinnamon (.25 tsp.)

Preparation Steps:

1. Heat up the coconut oil, milk, and almond butter in a small saucepan.
2. Once it's boiling, stir in the coconut and walnuts. Mix well and remove from the burner.
3. Let it cool about five minutes and serve.

Coffee Cake

Yields Provided: 8

Nutritional Facts Per Serving:

- 4 g Net Carbs
- 13 g Protein
- 28 g Total Fats
- 321 Calories

Ingredients Needed For The Base:

- Eggs (6 separated)
- Cream cheese (6 oz.)
- Erythritol (.25 cup)
- Liquid stevia (.25 tsp.)
- Unflavored protein powder (.25 cup)
- Cream of tartar (.25 tsp.)

- Vanilla extract (2 tsp.)

Ingredients Needed For The Filling:

- Cinnamon (1 tbsp.)
- Almond flour (1.5 cups)
- Butter (.5 stick)
- Maple Syrup Substitute (.25 cup)
- Erythritol (.25 cup)
- Also Needed: Dark metal cake pan

Preparation Steps:

1. Warm up the oven to 325° Fahrenheit.
2. Gently separate the egg whites from the yolks.
3. Whisk the egg yolks with the erythritol and add with the rest of the fixings. (Omit the egg whites and cream of tartar for the next step.)
4. Whisk the tartar and whites of the eggs to create stiff peaks. Gently work into the yolks.
5. Mix all of the filling fixings to form the dough.
6. Scoop the batter base into the pan. Top it off with ½ of the cinnamon filling, pushing it down if needed.
7. Bake for 20 minutes. Transfer to the countertop.
8. Prepare the cake with the rest of the filling dough.
9. Bake for another 20 minutes to half of an hour.
10. Cool for 10 to 20 minutes before serving.

Creamy Basil Baked Sausage

Yields Provided: 12

Nutritional Facts Per Serving:

- 4 g Net Carbs
- 23 g Protein
- 23 g Total Fats
- 316 Calories

Ingredients Needed:

- Italian sausage - pork/turkey or chicken (3 lb.)
- Cream cheese (8 oz.)
- Heavy cream (.25 cup)
- Basil pesto (.25 cup)
- Mozzarella (8 oz.)

Preparation Steps:

1. Warm up the oven to reach 400° Fahrenheit.
2. Lightly spritz a casserole dish with cooking oil spray. Add the sausage to the dish and bake for 30 minutes.
3. Combine the heavy cream, pesto, and cream cheese.
4. Once the sauce is done, pour it over the casserole and top it off with the cheese.
5. Bake for another 10 minutes. The sausage should reach 160° Fahrenheit in the center when checked with a

meat thermometer.

6. You can also broil for 3 minutes to brown the cheesy layer.

Flaxseed Waffles

Yields Provided: 4
Nutritional Facts Per Serving:
- 3.0 g Net Carbs
- 42 g Total Fats
- 18 g Protein
- 550 Calories

Ingredients Needed:
- Roughly ground flaxseed (2 cups)
- Baking powder - gluten-free (1 tbsp.)
- Sea salt (1 tsp.)
- Large eggs (5)
- Water (.5 cup)
- Avocado/Coconut or Extra-virgin olive oil (.33 cup)
- Ground cinnamon (2 tsp.)

Preparation Steps:
1. Warm up the waffle maker on the countertop using the medium heat setting.

2. Combine the baking powder, sea salt, and flaxseeds in a mixing container. Whisk well and set aside.

3. In a blender, add the oil, water, and eggs. Blend for 30 seconds until foamy. Pour the mixture into the bowl with flaxseeds.

4. Stir until just incorporated and allow to rest for 3 minutes.

5. At that time, stir in the cinnamon and pour into the waffle maker.

6. Serve right away or place in the freezer for a couple of weeks.

Ham Muffins

Yields Provided: 12

Nutritional Facts Per Serving:
- 1.5 g Net Carbs
- 10 g Protein
- 9 g Total Fats
- 129 Calories

Ingredients Needed:
- Ham (12 oz.)
- Green pepper (.25 cup)
- Celery (1 stalk)

- Pepper (1 tsp.)
- Onion powder (1 tsp.)
- Freshly chopped parsley (1 tbsp.)
- Minced chives (1 tbsp.)
- Dash of cayenne (1 dash)
- Shredded cheddar cheese (6 oz.)
- Eggs (3)

Preparation Steps:

1. Line a rimmed baking sheet with foil. Spritz the muffin tins with cooking oil spray.
2. Mince the celery and green pepper. Finely mince the ham in a food processor. Combine all of the fixings.
3. Spoon into the muffin tins sitting on the baking tin.
4. Warm up the oven to 350° Fahrenheit.
5. Bake for 30 to 35 minutes.
6. Remove when delicately browned.

High-Protein Yogurt Bowl

Yields Provided: 1

Nutritional Facts Per Serving:
- 9 g Net Carbs
- 13 g Protein
- 33 g Total Fats

- 274 Calories

Ingredients Needed:
- Plain yogurt (.5 cup)
- Sunflower seeds (.5 tbsp.)
- Walnuts (1 tbsp.)
- Chia seeds (.5 tbsp.)
- Protein powder (1 tbsp.)
- Coconut milk (.25 cup)
- Almond butter (1 tbsp.)

Preparation Steps:
1. Combine the yogurt, coconut milk, and protein powder in the blender.
2. Empty the mixture into a serving dish and add the walnuts, chia seeds, and sunflower seeds. Stir well.
3. Drizzle with the almond oil and serve.

Lemon Waffles

Yields Provided: 4
Nutritional Facts Per Serving:
- 2 g Net Carbs
- 1.1 g Protein
- 8 g Total Fats

- 99 Calories

Ingredients Needed:
- Coconut flour (.25 cup)
- Whole psyllium husks (1 tbsp.)
- Baking powder (.5 tsp.)
- Salt (1 pinch)
- Melted coconut butter (2 tbsp.) or Melted coconut oil (1.5 tbsp.)
- Granulated sweetener (1 tbsp.)
- Lemon juice (1 tbsp.)
- Nondairy milk of choice (5 tbsp.)
- Vanilla extract (.5 tsp.)

Preparation Steps:
1. Warm up a cast iron pan or ceramic non-stick pan using the med-low temperature setting. Grease the pan with additional coconut oil as needed.
2. Whisk the coconut flour, psyllium, baking powder, and salt.
3. Combine with the rest of the fixings in another container.
4. Gently fold in the dry fixings into the wet ones until thoroughly mixed. Let it rest until a stiff dough forms, about 3 to 5 minutes. Mold this with your

hands.

5. Tip: If the coconut oil and psyllium do not absorb enough liquid to form the dough, stir in an additional tablespoon of coconut flour.

6. Divide the dough into four portions and shape into dough balls.

7. Flatten the balls and cook for approximately five minutes per side, until golden.

8. Let cool for a minute or so before topping.

Oil-Free Blueberry Streusel Scones

Yields Provided: 12

Nutritional Facts Per Serving:

- 3.3 g Net Carbs
- 12 g Total Fats
- 0.6 g Protein
- 145 Calories

Ingredients Needed - The Scones:

- Almond flour (2 cups)
- Baking powder (1 tsp.)
- Ground stevia leaf (.25 tsp.)
- Salt (1 pinch)
- Fresh blueberries (1 cup)

- Egg (1)
- Almond milk (2 tbsp.)

Ingredients Needed - The Streusel Topping:
- Egg white (1 tbsp.)
- Slivered almonds (.25 cup)
- Ground cinnamon (.5 tsp.)
- Stevia (1 pinch)

Preparation Steps:
1. Warm up the oven to reach 375° Fahrenheit.
2. Prepare a cookie sheet with parchment baking paper or use a silicone baking mat.
3. Mix all of the fixings for the streusel in a small mixing bowl.
4. In a large bowl, combine the flour, stevia, salt, and baking powder. Whisk well to mix.
5. Stir in the blueberries and cover with the flour mixture. Set to the side for now.
6. Whisk the egg and milk together and add with the flour mixture. Stir well. Knead the dough and shape into 12 small scones about ½-inch thick.
7. Place on the prepared pan and bake for 20 to 22 minutes.
8. Cool 10 minutes and serve.

Omelet Wrap With Avocado & Salmon

Yields Provided: 2

Nutritional Facts Per Serving:

- 6 g Net Carbs
- 37 g Protein
- 67 g Total Fats
- 765 Calories

Ingredients Needed:

- Large eggs (3)
- Smoked salmon (1.8 oz.)
- Average-sized avocado (3.5 oz. or .5 of 1)
- Spring onion (1)
- Full-fat cream cheese (2 tbsp.)
- Freshly chopped chives (2 tbsp.)
- Butter or ghee (1 tbsp.)

Preparation Steps:

1. In a mixing bowl, add a pinch of pepper and salt along with the eggs. Whisk well. Fold in the chives and cream cheese.
2. Prepare the salmon and avocado; peel and slice.
3. In a skillet, add the butter or ghee to melt. Add the egg mixture and cook until fluffy. Put the omelet on a

serving dish and spoon the combination of cheese over it.

4. Sprinkle the onion, prepared avocado, and salmon into the wrap.

5. Close the prepared wrap and serve.

Pumpkin Pancakes

Yields Provided 1

Nutritional Facts Per Serving:
- 4 g Net Carbs
- 9 g Protein
- 56 g Total Fats
- 551 Calories

Ingredients Needed:
- Pumpkin puree (.25 cup)
- Eggs (2)
- Coconut flour (2 tbsp.)
- Cinnamon (.25 tsp.)
- Vanilla extract (.25 tsp.)
- Butter (2 tbsp.)
- Coconut oil (2 tbsp.)

Preparation Steps:

1. Whisk the eggs and puree with the cinnamon and vanilla extract.
2. Slowly, add the coconut flour, whisking until the lumps are gone.
3. Warm up the oil using the medium heat setting.
4. Once the pan is hot, prepare the pancakes until the first side starts to bubble.
5. Flip and continue cooking until golden brown. Serve with the butter.

Raspberry Breakfast Pudding Bowl

Yields Provided: 3
**Nutritional Facts Per Serving - **.5 cup each:

- 6 g Net Carbs
- 3 g Protein
- 34 g Total Fats
- 328 Calories

Ingredients Needed:

- Full-fat coconut milk (1.5 cups)
- Frozen raspberries (1 cup)
- MCT oil (.25 cup)
- Chia seeds (2 tbsp.)

- Apple cider vinegar (1 tbsp.)
- Alcohol-free stevia (3 drops)
- Vanilla extract (1 tsp.)
- *Optional:* Collagen (1 scoop)

Preparation Steps:

1. Combine all of the pudding fixings in the bowl of the food processor or jug of the blender.
2. Combine until creamy smooth.
3. Serve in a bowl (¾-cup size) and top with your favorites.
4. Serve with almonds, shredded coconut, fresh berries or hemp hearts. Remember to add the additional carbs.

Scallion Pancakes

Yields Provided: 4
Nutritional Facts Per Serving:
- 5 g Net Carbs
- 3 g Protein
- 16 g Total Fats
- 206 Calories

Ingredients Needed - The Pancakes:
- Coconut flour (.5 cup)

- Psyllium husk (2 tbsp.)
- Garlic powder (.5 tsp.)
- Salt (.25 tsp.)
- Scallions - white and green parts - sliced into thin rounds (2-3)
- Sesame oil (.25 cup)
- Warm water (1 cup)

Ingredients Needed - The Sauce:
- Tamari/Liquid aminos or soy sauce (1 tbsp.)
- Rice wine vinegar (1 tsp.)
- Water (1 tbsp.)
- Sesame oil - optional (1 tsp.)
- Finely minced garlic (1 clove)
- Chili flakes (to taste)

Preparation Steps:
1. Heat some sesame oil in a frying pan using medium-low heat.
2. Combine the water, oil, garlic, salt, scallions, and warm water. Let the mixture sit for about five minutes for the flavors to mix.
3. In another dish, whisk the coconut flour and psyllium husks.
4. Slowly add the water to the dry ingredients and let sit

for a minute until a dough forms. Separate the dough into four equal balls.

5. Flatten one ball in your hands into about a four-inch round. Place on skillet and flatten further with a spatula until it's about six inches in diameter. Fry for about five minutes on each side, until golden and crispy.

6. Repeat until done.

7. For the sauce - whisk ingredients together and serve.

Ultimate Eggs

Baked Eggs In The Avocado

Yields Provided: 1

Nutritional Facts Per Serving:

- 3.0 g Net Carbs
- 21 g Protein
- 52 g Total Fats
- 452 Calories

Ingredients Needed:

- Avocado (.5 of 1)
- Egg (1)
- Olive oil (1 tbsp.)
- Shredded cheddar cheese (.5 cup)

Preparation Steps:

1. Heat up the oven to 425° Fahrenheit.

2. Discard the avocado pit and remove just enough of the 'insides' to add the egg. Drizzle with the oil and break the egg into the shell.

3. Sprinkle with the cheese and bake for 15 to 16 minutes until the egg is the way you prefer. Serve.

Broccoli - Eggs & Sausage With Cheese

Yields Provided: 6

Nutritional Facts Per Serving:

*   4 g Net Carbs
*   26 g Protein
*   39 g Total Fats
*   484 Calories

Ingredients Needed:

*   Medium head of broccoli (1)
*   Low-carb sausage links (12. oz. pkg.)
*   Shredded cheddar cheese (1 cup - divided)
*   Eggs (10)
*   Whipping cream (.75 cup)
*   Minced garlic cloves (2)
*   Pepper (.25 tsp.)

- Salt (.5 tsp.)
- *Suggested Size:* 6-quart slow cooker

Preparation Steps:

1. Chop the broccoli. Mince the garlic and slice the sausage. Grease the pot with some non-stick cooking spray.
2. Layer the broccoli, sausage, and cheese in two-layer segments (6 layers total).
3. Combine the whipping cream, whisked eggs, salt, pepper, and garlic until well mixed. Add to the layered fixings.
4. Secure the lid and cook for two to three hours on high or for four to five hours on the low setting. The edges are browned, and the center is set when it is ready to serve.
5. *Note*: Make your own creation but count the carbs.

Cheesy Bacon & Egg Cups

Yields Provided: 6
Nutritional Facts Per Serving:
- 1 g Net Carbs
- 8 g Protein
- 7 g Total Fats

- 101 Calories

Ingredients Needed:

- Bacon (6 strips)
- Large eggs (6)
- Cheese (.25 cup)
- Fresh spinach (1 handful)
- Pepper & Salt (as desired)

Preparation Steps:

1. Set the oven setting to 400° Fahrenheit.
2. Prepare the bacon using medium heat on the stovetop. Place on towels to drain.
3. Grease six muffin tins with a spritz of oil. Line each tin with a slice of bacon, pressing tightly to make a secure well for the eggs.
4. Drain and dry the spinach with a paper towel. Whisk the eggs and combine with the spinach.
5. Add the mixture to the prepared tins and sprinkle with cheese. Sprinkle with salt and pepper until it's like you like it.
6. Bake for 15 minutes. Remove when done and serve or cool to store in the fridge.

Coconut Almond Egg Wraps

Yields Provided: 4

Nutritional Facts Per Serving:

- 3.0 g Net Carbs
- 8 g Protein
- 8 g Total Fats
- 111 Calories

Ingredients Needed:

- Organic eggs (5)
- Coconut flour (1 tbsp.)
- Sea salt (.25 tsp.)
- Almond meal (2 tbsp.)

Preparation Steps:

1. Combine the fixings in a blender and work until creamy.
2. Warm up a skillet using the med-high temperature setting.
3. Pour 2 tbsp. of batter into the pan and cook - covered about 3 minutes.
4. Flip it over and continue cooking for another 3 minutes.
5. Serve hot.

Cream Cheese Eggs

Yields Provided: 1

Nutritional Facts Per Serving:

- 3.0 g Net Carbs
- 15 g Protein
- 31 g Total Fats
- 341 Calories

Ingredients Needed:

- Butter (1 tbsp.)
- Eggs (2)
- Soft cream cheese with chives (2 tbsp.)

Preparation Steps:

1. Preheat a skillet and melt the butter.
2. Whisk the eggs with the cream cheese.
3. Add to the pan and stir until done.

Delicious Italian Omelet

Yields Provided: 1 large

Nutritional Facts Per Serving:

- 3.0 g Net Carbs
- 33 g Protein

- 36 g Total Fats
- 451 Calories

Ingredients Needed:
- Eggs (2)
- Water (1 tbsp.)
- Butter or ghee (1 tbsp.)
- Thin slices salami/prosciutto (3)
- Basil leaves (6)
- Mozzarella cheese slices (2 oz.)
- Thin slices of tomato (5)
- Pepper and salt (as desired)

Preparation Steps:
1. Toss the ghee or butter in a frying pan using the medium heat setting to melt.
2. Whisk the water and eggs together. Pour into the hot pan and cook for about 30 seconds.
3. Spread out the meat slices over top of the egg followed by the cheese, tomatoes, and slices of basil. Season with the salt and pepper.
4. Cook approximately two minutes or until firm. Flip and cook an additional minute before folding in half.
5. Cover the pan and simmer over low heat.
6. When the center is done, add the omelet to a plate and

serve.

Mushroom Omelet

Yields Provided: 1

Nutritional Facts Per Serving:

- 3.0 g Net Carbs
- 24 g Protein
- 55 g Total Fats
- 490 Calories

Ingredients Needed:

- Egg (1)
- Cheddar (.5 cup)
- Butter (1.5 tbsp.)
- Green onion (1 tbsp.)
- White mushrooms (.25 cup)
- Heavy cream (2 tbsp.)

Preparation Steps:

1. Chop the mushrooms and onion.
2. Whisk the heavy cream and egg together with a sprinkle of the pepper and salt as desired.
3. Warm up a small pan and add .5 tablespoon of the butter. Toss in the mushroom and saute for about 7

minutes or until lightly browned.

4. Stir in the whisked egg and cheese.

5. Garnish with the chopped onions and serve.

Spinach & Ham Mini Quiche

Yields Provided: 2

Nutritional Facts Per Serving:

- 2 g Net Carbs
- 20 g Protein
- 13 g Total Fats
- 210 Calories

Ingredients Needed:

- Diced ham (4 slices)
- Whisked eggs (3)
- Chopped spinach (.75 cup)
- Chopped leek (.25 cup)
- Coconut milk (.25 cup)
- Baking powder (.5 tsp.)
- Pepper & salt (to your liking)

Preparation Steps:

1. Warm up the oven temperature to 350° Fahrenheit.

2. Combine all of the fixings in a large mixing container.

3. Pour the mixture into tart pans or four small mini quiche pans.

4. Bake 15 minutes. Serve.

Tomato & Cheese Frittata

Yields Provided: 2

Nutritional Facts Per Serving:
- 6 g Net Carbs
- 27 g Protein
- 33 g Total Fats
- 435 Calories

Ingredients Needed:
- Eggs (6)
- Soft cheese (3.5 oz. or .66 cup)
- White onion (.5 of 1 medium)
- Halved cherry tomatoes (.66 cup)
- Chopped herbs - ex. basil or chives (2 tbsp.)
- Ghee or butter (1 tbsp.)

Preparation Steps:
1. Set the oven broiler temperature to 400° Fahrenheit.
2. Arrange the onions on a greased and hot iron skillet. Cook with either the ghee or butter until lightly

browned.

3. In another dish, crack the eggs and flavor with the salt, pepper, or add some herbs of your choice. Whisk and add to the pan of onions, cooking until the edges begin to get crispy.

4. Top with the cheese (such as feta), and a few diced tomatoes. Put the pan in the broiler for five to seven minutes or until done.

5. Enjoy piping hot or let cool down.

6. *Note*: You can purge all of the leftover veggies into the recipe (if you wish).

Delicious Beverages

Bulletproof Coffee

Yields Provided: 1

Nutritional Facts Per Serving:

- 0 g Net Carbs
- 1 g Protein
- 51 g Total Fats
- 463 Calories

Ingredients Needed:

- MCT oil powder (2 tbsp.)

- Ghee or butter (2 tbsp.)
- Hot coffee (1.5 cups)

Preparation Steps:

1. Prepare and pour the hot coffee into your blender.
2. Add in the powder and ghee/butter. Blend until frothy.
3. Serve in a large mug.

Coffee & Cream

Yields Provided: 1

Nutritional Facts Per Serving:

- 2 g Net Carbs
- 22 g Total Fats
- 206 Calories

Ingredients Needed:

- Coffee brewed to your liking (.75 cup)
- Heavy whipping cream (4 tbsp.)

Preparation Steps:

1. Prepare your coffee the way you want it.
2. Add the cream to a saucepan. Heat until it's frothy.
3. Pour the cream into a large mug, add the coffee, and stir.

4. Serve and enjoy with a slice of cheese and a handful of nuts for a snack or as it is.

Hot Chocolate

Yields Provided: 1

Nutritional Facts Per Serving:
- 1 g Net Carbs
- 1 g Protein
- 23 g Total Fats
- 216 Calories

Ingredients Needed:
- Cocoa powder (1 tbsp.)
- Unsalted butter (1 oz.)
- Vanilla extract (.25 tsp.)
- Boiling water (1 cup)
- Powdered erythritol - optional (1 tsp.)
- *Also Needed*: Immersion blender

Preparation Steps:
1. Add each of the ingredients into a tall container to prepare using the blender.
2. Mix for about 15 to 20 seconds until the foam is no longer on the top.

3. Pour the cocoa into the cups and serve.

Chapter 4: Keto Lunch: Salads - Soups & Pasta

Salad Choices:

Asian Zucchini Salad

Yields Provided: 1

Nutritional Facts Per Serving:

- 7 g Net Carbs
- 14 g Protein

- 86 g Total Fats
- 846 Calories

Ingredients Needed:
- Medium zucchini (1)
- Shredded cabbage (.5 cup)
- Sunflower seeds (1.5 tbsp.)
- Almonds (.5 tbsp.)
- Sesame oil (1.5 tbsp.)
- White vinegar (1 tbsp.)
- Crumbled feta cheese (.5 cup)

Preparation Steps:
1. Roast the almonds in a deep frying pan using the low-temperature setting.
2. Use a spiralizer to shred the zucchini into strips.
3. Prepare the salad using the cabbage, zucchini, almonds, and sunflower seeds.
4. Whisk both oils and the vinegar and spritz over the salad.
5. Garnish with the feta and toss before serving.

Avocado - Corn Salad

Yields Provided: 4

Nutritional Facts Per Serving:

- 4.5 g Net Carbs
- 3.5 g Protein
- 11 g Total Fats
- 147 Calories

Ingredients Needed - The Salad:

- Cooked - corn on the cob - husk removed (1)
- Romaine head (1 chopped)
- Quartered grape tomatoes (4)
- Sliced red onion (.25 cup)
- Sliced avocado (.5 of 1)

Ingredients Needed - The Dressing:

- Minced shallots (1 tbsp.)
- Dijon mustard (2 tsp.)
- White wine vinegar (2 tbsp.)
- 1% Vegan buttermilk (6 tbsp.)
- Garlic powder (.25 tsp.)
- Kosher salt (.5 tsp.)
- Black pepper (1 pinch)
- Extra-Virgin olive oil (2 tbsp.)

Preparation Steps:

1. Whisk each of the dressing components and place in a serving jar.
2. Combine the salad fixings in a large salad bowl and toss with the dressing.

Crunchy Cauliflower & Pine Nut Salad

Yields Provided: 1

Nutritional Facts Per Serving:

- 8 g Net Carbs
- 10 g Protein
- 63 g Total Fats
- 638 Calories

Ingredients Needed:

- Cauliflower (.25 cup)
- Onion leeks (2 tbsp.)
- Pine nuts (.25 cup)
- Sour cream (2 tbsp.)
- Iceberg lettuce (.5 cup)
- Mayonnaise (.25 cup)
- Feta cheese (.25 cup)

Preparation Steps:

1. Chop the cauliflower, onion, and pine nuts. Shred the lettuce.
2. Toast the pine nuts using the medium heat setting.
3. Combine all of the fixings in a large container and place in the fridge for a minimum of two hours.
4. Serve cold.

Feta Cheese Salad With Balsamic Butter

Yields Provided: 1

Nutritional Facts Per Serving:

- 8 g Net Carbs
- 16 g Protein
- 70 g Total Fats
- 609 Calories

Ingredients Needed:

- Baby spinach (.5 cup)
- Crumbled feta cheese (.5 cup)
- Pumpkin seeds (.125 cup)
- Butter (.25 cup)
- Balsamic vinegar (1 tbsp.)

Preparation Steps:

1. Warm up the oven to reach 400° Fahrenheit.
2. Crumble the cheese on a greased baking tray. Bake for about 10 minutes.
3. Use the high-temperature setting on the stovetop to heat a dry skillet. Toast the seeds until they begin to pop.
4. Reduce the temperature and add the butter. Simmer until golden brown and add the vinegar. Simmer for about two minutes and turn off the burner.
5. Arrange the baby spinach leaves on a salad dish.
6. Pour the butter over that and top it with the feta cheese before serving.

Ginger Walnut & Hemp Seed Lettuce Wraps

Yields Provided: 4
Nutritional Facts Per Serving:

- 10 g Net Carbs
- 14 g Protein
- 31 g Total Fats
- 382 Calories

Ingredients Needed - The Sauce:

- Low-sodium tamari (2 tbsp.)

- Maple syrup (1 tbsp.)
- Brown rice vinegar (2 tbsp.)
- Minced ginger (1 tbsp.)
- Toasted sesame oil (1 tsp.)

Ingredients Needed - The Filling:

- Hemp seeds (.5 cup)
- Walnuts (1 cup)
- Dates (2)
- Cucumber (.5 cup)
- Carrots (.25 cup)
- Lettuce leaves
- *Optional:* Sesame seeds

Preparation Steps:

1. Mix the sauce fixings and set aside.
2. Chop the dates, walnuts, carrots, and cucumbers.
3. Combine the sauce with the rest of the filling ingredients. Place in the refrigerator to chill for one hour.
4. Remove and pile onto the leaves of lettuce and top off with the seeds as desired.

Jar Salad

Yields Provided: 1

Nutritional Facts Per Serving:

- 4 g Net Carbs
- 8 g Protein
- 19 g Total Fats
- 215 Calories

Ingredients Needed:

- Black pepper & Salt (as desired)
- Keto-friendly mayonnaise (4 tbsp.)
- Scallion (.5)
- Cucumber (.25 oz.)
- Red bell pepper (.25 oz.)
- Cherry tomatoes (.25 oz.)
- Leafy greens (.25 oz.)
- Seasoned tempeh (4 oz.)

Preparation Steps:

1. Chop or shred the vegetables as desired.
2. Layer in the dark leafy greens first, followed by the onions, tomato, bell peppers, avocado, and shredded carrot.
3. Top with the tempeh, or use the same amount of

another high-protein option to mix things up in later weeks.

4. Top with keto-vegan mayonnaise prior to serving.

Keto Salad Nicoise

Yields Provided: 1

Nutritional Facts Per Serving:
- 8 g Net Carbs
- 18 g Protein
- 48 g Total Fats
- 544 Calories

Ingredients Needed:
- Large egg (1)
- Celery (.5 cup)
- Snow peas (.5 cup)
- Olive oil (2 tbsp.)
- Garlic (.25 tbsp.)
- Romaine lettuce (1 cup)
- Green onion (.5 tbsp.)
- Olives (.5 tbsp.)
- Crumbled feta cheese (.5 cup)
- Balsamic vinegar (1 tbsp.)

Preparation Steps:

1. Hard boil the egg and remove the peel when cooled.

2. Chop the garlic, onion, celery, and olives.

3. Pour the olive oil into a small pan. Sauté the garlic, olives, and snow peas until the peas are bright green.

4. Prepare a large salad bowl and add the cooked veggies, shredded lettuce, celery, and green onion.

5. Make the dressing by whisking the vinegar and oil with the salt and pepper.

6. Combine the fixings and toss well before serving.

Salad Sandwich

Yields Provided: 1

Nutritional Facts Per Serving:

- 4.5 g Net Carbs
- 4 g Protein
- 15 g Total Fats
- 104 Calories

Ingredients Needed:

- Butter (.5 oz.)
- Romaine or baby gem lettuce (2 oz.)
- Adam cheese (1 oz.)
- Cherry tomato (1 sliced)

- Sliced avocado (.5 of 1)

Preparation Steps:

1. Rinse the lettuce and slice the rest of the ingredients.
2. Add butter on the leaves with a layer of cheese, avocado, and tomato. Top it off with lettuce and serve.

Steak Salad

Yields Provided: 2
Nutritional Facts Per Serving:

- 1.5 g Net Carbs
- 25 g Protein
- 33 g Total Fats
- 403 Calories

Ingredients Needed:

- Ribeye steak (1- 8 oz.)
- Green salad mix (2 cups)
- Steakhouse seasoning (1 tbsp.)
- Olive oil (1 tbsp.)
- Wine vinegar (1 tsp.)
- Pepper and salt (to taste)

Preparation Steps:

1. Use the steak seasoning to prepare the steak and cook to your liking. Let it rest until cooled.
2. Arrange all of the salad fixings and sprinkle with the pepper and salt.
3. Toss and drizzle with the oil.
4. Slice the steak into bite-sized strips.
5. Place the salad on two serving dishes and sprinkle the steak bits on top.
6. Use your favorite dressing if desired - but count the carbs.

Soup Options:

Asiago Tomato Soup

Yields Provided: 4

Nutritional Facts Per Serving:

- 8.75 g Net Carbs
- 9 g Protein
- 26 g Total Fats
- 302 Calories

Ingredients Needed:

- Tomato paste (1 small can)

- Minced garlic (1 tsp.)
- Oregano (1 tsp.)
- Heavy whipping cream (1 cup)
- Water (.25 cup)
- Pepper and salt (as desired)
- Asiago cheese (.75 cup)

Preparation Steps:

1. Pour the minced garlic and tomato paste in a dutch oven and add the cream. Gently whisk.
2. As it begins to boil, blend in small amounts of cheese. Pour in the water and simmer 4 to 5 minutes.
3. Serve with pepper as desired.

Avocado Mint Chilled Soup

Yields Provided: 2
Nutritional Facts Per Serving:
- 4 g Net Carbs
- 4 g Protein
- 26 g Total Fats
- 280 Calories

Ingredients Needed:
- Romaine lettuce (2 leaves)
- Ripened avocado (1 medium)

- Coconut milk (1 cup)
- Lime juice (1 tbsp.)
- Fresh mint (20 leaves)
- Salt (to your liking)

Preparation Steps:

1. Combine all of the fixings into a blender and mix well. You want it thick but not puree-like.
2. Chill in the refrigerator for 5-10 minutes before serving.

Beef Curry - Slow-Cooked

Yields Provided: 8

Nutritional Facts Per Serving:

- 5 g Net Carbs
- 26 g Protein
- 22 g Total Fats
- 351 Calories

Ingredients Needed:

- Chuck roast (2.5 lb.)
- Coconut milk powder (6 tbsp.)
- Water (2 cups)
- Red curry paste (3 tbsp.)
- Cardamom pods (5 cracked)

- Dried Thai chilis/fresh red chilis (2 tbsp.)
- Thai fish sauce (2 tbsp.)
- Ground cloves (.125 tsp.)
- Nutmeg (.125 tsp.)
- Dried onion flakes (1 tbsp.)
- Ground coriander (1 tbsp.)
- Ginger (1 tbsp.)
- Cumin (1 tbsp.)
- Granulated sugar substitute (1 tbsp.)

Ingredients Needed For Serving:

- Coconut milk powder (2 tbsp.)
- Granulated sugar substitute (2 tbsp.)
- Red curry paste (1 tbsp.)
- Fresh cilantro (.25 cup)
- Cashews (.25 cup or can omit)
- *Optional*: Xanthan gum .25 tsp.)

Preparation Steps:

1. Place the meat in the slow cooker. Pour in the milk, water, fish sauce, curry paste, ginger, cloves, nutmeg, coriander, cumin, your chosen sweetener, the onion flakes, chilis, and cardamom pods.
2. Place the top on the slow cooker. Use the low setting for eight hours or high for five hours.

3. Right before serving, place the meat on a platter. Whisk the sauce with two tablespoons of the milk powder, the xanthan gum, sugar substitute sweetener, and curry paste.
4. Tear the meat to shreds and stir into the sauce. Garnish with some cilantro and serve. Enjoy with your favorite sides but be sure to add the carbs.

Broccoli & Cheese Soup

Yields Provided: 4
Nutritional Facts Per Serving:
- 10 g Net Carbs
- 24 g Protein
- 52 g Total Fats
- 561 Calories

Ingredients Needed:
- Small diced onion (1)
- Chopped broccoli (4 cups)
- Vegetable stock (1.5 cups)
- Minced garlic (1 tsp.)
- Shredded sharp cheddar cheese (3 cups)
- Pepper & salt (to your liking)
- Heavy cream (.75 cup)

Preparation Steps:

1. Use the medium heat setting on the stovetop to warm a skillet. Toss in the broccoli, onions, and garlic. Saute for about five minutes.

2. Once boiling, cover, and simmer for another ten minutes.

3. Pour in the heavy cream and cook for three to five minutes.

4. Fold in the cheese and stir until creamy smooth or around one to two minutes. Give it a shake of salt and pepper. Serve.

Cabbage Roll 'Unstuffed' Soup

Yields Provided: 9

Nutritional Facts Per Serving:

- 3.3 g Net Carbs
- 16 g Protein
- 15 g Total Fats
- 217 Calories

Ingredients Needed:

- Minced garlic cloves (2)
- Small diced onion (.5 of 1)
- 80/20 Ground beef (1.5 lb.)

- Bragg's Aminos (.25 cup)
- Tomato sauce (8 oz. can)
- Beef broth (3 cups)
- Keto-friendly Worcestershire sauce/another substitute (3 tsp.)
- Diced tomatoes (14 oz. can)
- Chopped cabbage (1 medium)
- Pepper (.5 tsp.)
- Parsley (.5 tsp.)
- Salt (.5 tsp.
- *Also Needed:* Instant Pot

Preparation Steps:

1. Prepare using the saute function on the Instant Pot to brown the beef, garlic, and onions.
2. Drain and add back to the pot with the rest of the fixings.
3. Program the unit on the soup function.
4. Natural release the soup for about ten minutes, and quick release the rest of the steam. Stir and serve.

Carrot & Beef Soup

Yields Provided: 4
Nutritional Facts Per Serving:

- 3.0 g Net Carbs

- 25 g Protein
- 65 g Total Fats
- 328 Calories

Ingredients Needed:

- Beef stew meat (2 lb.)
- Pepper & Salt (as desired)
- Cooking oil (2 tbsp.)
- Tomato paste (1 tbsp.)
- Garlic cloves (4)
- Sliced onion (1)
- Sliced carrots (4 peeled)
- Beef broth (3 cups)
- Bay leaves (2)
- Thyme sprigs (6)
- Water (1 cup)

Preparation Steps:

1. Dust the salt and pepper over the chopped beef.
2. Warm up the Instant Pot using the saute function. Pour in the oil and add the beef. Saute for 4 to 5 minutes until browned.
3. Stir in the onions, garlic, and carrots. Simmer 2 minutes and toss in the bay leaves, thyme, broth, and tomato paste. Stir well.

4. Secure the lid and set the time for 30 minutes – manual setting.
5. When the time is elapsed; natural release the pressure for 8-10 minutes and open the lid.
6. Season and enjoy warm.

Chili Delight - No-Beans

Yields Provided: 6

Nutritional Facts Per Serving:
- 5 g Net Carbs
- 26 g Protein
- 14 g Total Fats
- 263 Calories

Ingredients Needed:
- Water (3 cups)
- Ground beef 1.5 lb.)
- Cumin (.75 tsp.)
- Black pepper (.75 tsp.)
- Cinnamon (.25 tsp.)
- Minced garlic cloves (2)
- Chopped onion (.25 cup)
- Worcestershire sauce (1 tsp.)
- Bay leaves (3)

- Chili powder (2 tbsp.)
- Salt (1.5 tsp.)
- Allspice (.5 tsp.)
- Red pepper (.5 tsp.)
- Tomato paste (6 oz.)
- Sliced black olives (2.25 oz.)
- Finely chopped chili peppers (.25 cup)

Preparation Steps:

1. Break apart the ground beef in a large stew pot on the stovetop. Drain away the juices.
2. Combine with the rest of the fixings. Bring to a boil.
3. Simmer two hours and serve.

Chili & Steak Explosion

Yields Provided: 12

Nutritional Facts Per Serving - With Toppings:
- 13.5 g Net Carbs
- 33 g Protein
- 41 g Total Fats
- 540 Calories

Nutritional Facts Per Serving - Without Toppings:
- 3.0 g Net Carbs
- 38 g Protein

- 26 g Total Fats
- 321 Calories

Ingredients Needed - The Chili:
- Beef/chicken stock (1 cup)
- Steak of choice (2.5 lb.)
- Sliced leeks (.5 cup)
- Whole tomatoes - canned with juices (2 cups)
- Salt (.5 tsp.)
- Cumin (.5 tsp.)
- Chili powder (1 tbsp.)
- Black pepper (.125 tsp.)
- Ground cayenne pepper (.25 tsp.)

Ingredients Needed - Optional Toppings:
- Avocado – sliced or cubed (.5 of 1)
- Sour cream (2 tbsp.)
- Freshly chopped cilantro (1 tsp.)
- Shredded cheddar cheese (.25 cup)

Preparation Steps:
1. Slice the steak into 1-inch cubes.
2. Combine all of the fixings into the cooker - except for the toppings.
3. Use the high setting on the slow cooker for about six

hours.

4. Serve and enjoy.

Creamy Chicken Soup

Yields Provided: 4

Nutritional Facts Per Serving:

- 2 g Net Carbs
- 18 g Protein
- 25 g Total Fats
- 307 Calories

Ingredients Needed:

- Butter (2 tbsp.)
- Chicken (1 large breast or 2 cups shredded)
- Cream cheese (4 oz.)
- Garlic seasoning (2 tbsp.)
- Chicken broth (14.5 oz.)
- Salt (as desired)
- Heavy cream (.25 cup)

Preparation Steps:

1. Heat up a saucepan and melt the butter using the medium heat setting.
2. Shred and add the chicken. Cube and fold in the cream cheese and seasoning. Stir well.

3. When melted, add the heavy cream and broth.

4. Lower the heat setting once the cheese and broth start boiling. Simmer for 3 to 4 minutes. Season as desired.

Egg Drop Soup

Yields Provided: 6

Nutritional Facts Per Serving:
- 3.0 g Net Carbs
- 11 g Protein
- 22 g Total Fats
- 255 Calories

Ingredients Needed:
- Vegetable broth (2 quarts)
- Freshly chopped ginger (1 tbsp.)
- Turmeric (1 tbsp.)
- Sliced chili pepper (1 small)
- Coconut aminos (2 tbsp.)
- Minced garlic cloves (2)
- Large eggs (4)
- Mushrooms (2 cups sliced)
- Chopped spinach (4 cups)
- Sliced spring onions (2 medium)
- Freshly chopped cilantro (2 tbsp.)

- Black pepper (to your liking)
- Pink Himalayan (1 tsp.)
- For serving: Olive oil (6 tbsp.)

Preparation Steps:

1. Prep the Fixings: Grate the ginger root and turmeric. Mince the garlic cloves and slice the peppers and mushrooms.
2. Chop the chard stalks and leaves. Separate the stalks from the leaves. Dump the vegetable stock into a soup pot and simmer until it begins to boil. Toss in the garlic, ginger, turmeric, chard stalks, mushrooms, coconut aminos, and chili peppers. Boil for approximately five minutes.
3. Fold in the chard leaves and simmer for one minute.
4. Whip the eggs in a dish and add them slowly to the soup mixture. Stir until the egg is done and set it on the counter.
5. Slice the onions and chop the cilantro. Toss them into the pot.
6. Pour into serving bowls and drizzle with some olive oil (1 tbsp. per serving).
7. Serve warm or chilled.

Greens Soup

Yields Provided: 6

Nutritional Facts Per Serving:

- 6 g Net Carbs
- 6 g Protein
- 8 g Total Fats
- 191 Calories

Ingredients Needed:

- Spinach leaves (2 cups)
- Diced avocado (1)
- Diced English cucumber (.5 cup)
- Gluten-free vegetable broth (.25 cup)
- Black pepper and salt (as desired)

Preparation Steps:

1. Combine each of the fixings in the blender.
2. Toss in the fresh herbs and serve.

Mexican Chicken Soup

Yields Provided: 6

Nutritional Facts Per Serving:

- 5 g Net Carbs

- 28 g Protein
- 23 g Total Fats
- 400 Calories

Ingredients Needed:

- Chicken thighs (1.5 lb.)
- Chicken broth (15 oz.)
- Pepper Jack/Monterey cheese (8 oz.)
- Chunky salsa – ex. Tostitos (15.5 oz.)
- Also Needed: Slow Cooker

Preparation Steps:

1. Cut out any bones and remove the fat from the chicken. Arrange them in the slow cooker.
2. Mix in the rest of the fixings. Prepare using the low setting (6-8 hrs.) or the high setting (3 to 4 hrs.).
3. When the time is up, remove and shred the chicken. Put it back in the cooker to mingle with the juices for a minute or so.
4. Stir and serve - right out of the cooker.

Tomato Soup

Yields Provided: 8
Nutritional Facts Per Serving:

- 6.5 g Net Carbs
- 11 g Protein
- 18 g Total Fats
- 300 Calories

Ingredients Needed:

- Coconut cream (1 cup)
- Veggie broth (29 oz.)
- Tomatoes (3 lb.)
- Diced onion (1)
- Vegan butter or your choice (3 tbsp.)

Preparation Steps:

1. Warm up the Instant Pot using the saute mode. Once it's hot, add the butter to melt and toss in the onions. Saute for 3 to 5 minutes.
2. Stir in the tomatoes and simmer for another 2 minutes.
3. Secure the lid and set the soup function for 6 minutes.
4. Press the cancel button and wait about 4 to 5 minutes before you quick release the pressure. Stir in the coconut cream to saute for 1 minute.
5. Use a hand blender to puree the soup and serve.

Pasta - Rice & 'Zoodle' Choices:

Baked Zucchini Noodles With Feta

Yields Provided: 3
Nutritional Facts Per Serving:

- 5 g Net Carbs
- 4 g Protein
- 8 g Total Fats
- 105 Calories

Ingredients Needed:

- Quartered plum tomato (1)
- Spiralized zucchini (2)
- Feta cheese (8 cubes)
- Pepper and salt (1 tsp. each)
- Olive oil (1 tbsp.)

Preparation Steps:

1. Lightly grease a roasting pan with a spritz of oil.
2. Set the oven temperature to reach 375° Fahrenheit.
3. Slice the noodles with a spiralizer and add to the prepared pan along with the olive oil and tomatoes. Sprinkle with the pepper and salt.
4. Bake for 10 to 15 minutes. Transfer from the oven and

add the cheese cubes, tossing to combine. Serve.

Creamy Salmon & Pasta

Yields Provided: 2

Nutritional Facts Per Serving:

- 3.0 g Net Carbs
- 21 g Protein
- 42 g Total Fats
- 470 Calories

Ingredients Needed:

- Coconut oil (2 tbsp.)
- Zucchinis (2)
- Smoked salmon (8 oz.)
- Keto-friendly mayo (.25 cup)

Preparation Steps:

1. Use a peeler or spiralizer to make noodle-like strands from the zucchini.
2. Warm up the oil over the med-high temperature setting. When hot, add the salmon and saute 2 to 3 minutes until golden brown.
3. Stir in the noodles and saute 1 to 2 more minutes.
4. Store the noodles in the fridge after cooled overnight.

5. When it's time to eat, just stir in the mayo and divide the pasta between two dishes. Serve.

Marinara Zoodles

Yields Provided: 4

Nutritional Facts Per Serving:

- 5 g Net Carbs
- 7 g Protein
- 19 g Total Fats
- 179 Calories

Ingredients Needed:

- Extra-Virgin olive oil (2 tbsp.)
- Garlic cloves (6)
- White onions (.5 cup)
- Tomatoes (14 oz.)
- Tomato paste (2 tbsp.)
- Basil leaves (.5 cup - loosely packed)
- Coarse salt (1.5 tsp.)
- Freshly ground black pepper (.25 tsp.)
- Cayenne (1 pinch)
- Spiralized zucchinis (2 large)

Preparation Steps:

1. Pour the oil into the skillet before placing it on the stovetop (medium heat setting).

2. Mince the garlic cloves, onions, and tomatoes. Roughly chop the basil leaves. Use a veggie peeler, knife, or spiralizer to prepare the zucchini.

3. Toss in and sauté the onion for about five minutes before adding in the garlic. Cook approximately 60 seconds.

4. Mix in the salt, crushed red pepper flakes, pepper, salt, basil, tomato paste, and tomatoes. Combine thoroughly.

5. Simmer the sauce and lower the temperature setting to medium-low. Simmer an additional 15 minutes or until the oil takes on a deep orange color which indicates the sauce is thickened and reduced. Season as desired.

6. Add in the zoodles and let them soften approximately two minutes before serving.

Thai-Inspired Peanut Red Curry Vegan Bowl

Yields Provided: 1

Nutritional Facts Per Serving:

- 10 g Net Carbs
- 16 g Protein

- 23 g Total Fats
- 355 Calories

Ingredients Needed:

- Sesame oil (1 tsp.)
- Shirataki noodles (8 oz. pkg.)
- Unsweetened peanut butter (2 tbsp.)
- Low-sodium tamari (2 tsp.)
- Thai red curry paste (2-3 tsp.)
- Grated ginger (.25 tsp.)
- Fresh edamame (.25 cup)
- Fresh lime juice (1 tsp.)

Optional Garnishes Needed:

- Red pepper flakes (1 pinch)
- Chopped peanuts
- Additional lime juice

Preparation Steps:

1. Thoroughly rinse and drain the noodles and add to a frying pan using the medium-low temperature setting. Cook for a few minutes until the noodles are mostly dry.
2. Stir in the curry paste, tamari, peanut butter, sesame oil, grated ginger, and bell peppers. Stir until a sauce

forms and everything is evenly coated.

3. Simmer for about three to five more minutes or until the peppers soften and everything is heated through.

4. Transfer the hot curry to a bowl and top with edamame and other desired toppings.

Chapter 5: Keto Dinner Favorites: Fish & Poultry

Fish Choices:

Bacon & Shrimp Risotto

Yields Provided: 2

Nutritional Facts Per Serving:

- 5 g Net Carbs
- 24 g Protein
- 9 g Total Fats

- 224 Calories

Ingredients Needed:
- Bacon (4 slices)
- Daikon winter radish (2 cups)
- Dry white wine (2 tbsp.)
- Chicken stock (.25 cup)
- Garlic (1 clove)
- Ground pepper (to your liking)
- Chopped parsley (2 tbsp.)
- Cooked shrimp (4 oz.)

Preparation Steps:
1. Peel and slice the radish, mince the garlic, and chop the bacon. Remove as much water as possible from the daikon once it's shredded.
2. On the stovetop, heat up a saucepan using the medium heat temperature setting. Toss in the bacon and fry until it's crispy. Leave the drippings in the pan and remove the bacon with a slotted spoon to drain.
3. Add the stock, wine, daikon, salt, pepper, and garlic into the pan. Simmer for 6-8 minutes until most of the liquid is absorbed.
4. Fold in the bacon (saving a few bits for the topping), and shrimp along with the parsley. Serve.

5. *Tip*: If you cannot find the daikon, just substitute it using shredded cauliflower.

Sesame Ginger Salmon

Yields Provided: 2

Nutritional Facts Per Serving:

- 2.5 g Net Carbs
- 33 g Protein
- 24 g Total Fats
- 370 Calories

Ingredients Needed:

- Salmon fillet (10 oz.)
- Sesame oil (2 tsp.)
- White wine (2 tbsp.)
- Soy sauce (2 tbsp.)
- Minced ginger (1-2 tsp.)
- Rice vinegar (1 tbsp.)
- Sugar-free ketchup (1 tbsp.)
- Fish sauce - ex. Red Boat (1 tbsp.)

Preparation Steps:

1. Combine all of the fixings in a plastic container with a tight-fitting lid, omitting the ketchup, oil, and wine for

now. Marinade for about 10 to 15 minutes.

2. On the stovetop, prepare a skillet using the high heat temperature setting and pour in the oil. Add the fish when it's hot with the skin side facing down.

3. Brown both sides for three to four minutes. When you flip it over, pour in the marinated juices and simmer. Arrange the fish on two dinner plates.

4. Add the wine and ketchup to the pan and simmer five minutes until it's reduced. Serve with your favorite side dish.

Shrimp Alfredo

Yields Provided: 4

Nutritional Facts Per Serving:

- 6.5 g Net Carbs
- 23 g Protein
- 18 g Total Fats
- 298 Calories

Ingredients Needed:

- Raw shrimp (1 lb.)
- Salted butter (1 tbsp.)
- Cubed cream cheese (4 oz.)
- Whole milk (.5 cup)

- Salt (1 tsp.)
- Dried basil (1 tsp.)
- Garlic powder (1 tbsp.)
- Shredded parmesan cheese (.5 cup)
- Baby kale or spinach (.25 cup)
- Whole sun-dried tomatoes (5)

Preparation Steps:

1. Heat up the butter using the medium heat setting in a skillet.
2. Toss in the shrimp and lower the heat to medium-low. After 30 seconds, flip the shrimp and cook until slightly pink. Blend in the cream cheese.
3. Increase the heat and pour in the milk. Stir frequently.
4. Sprinkle with the salt, basil, and garlic. Empty the parmesan cheese in and mix well.
5. Simmer until the sauce has thickened. Cut the sun-dried tomatoes into strips.
6. Lastly, fold in the kale/spinach and dried tomatoes. Serve steaming hot.

Poultry Choices:

Cheesy Bacon Chicken

Yields Provided: 6

Nutritional Facts Per Serving:
- 1 g Net Carbs
- 29 g Protein
- 23 g Total Fats
- 345 Calories

Ingredients Needed:
- Chicken breasts - cut in half widthwise (2.5-3 lbs. or 5 to 6)
- Seasoning rub/seasoning salt or a mix of salt, garlic powder, onion powder, paprika (2 tbsp.)
- Bacon - cut strips in half (.5 lb.)
- Shredded cheddar (4 oz.)
- Sugar-free barbecue sauce - optional for serving

Preparation Steps:
1. Warm up the oven to reach 400° Fahrenheit.
2. Spray a large rimmed baking sheet with cooking spray.
3. Rub both sides of chicken breasts with seasoning rub.
4. Top each with a piece of bacon. Bake for 30 min on the

top rack until the chicken is 160° Fahrenheit and the bacon looks crispy.

5. Remove tray from the oven and sprinkle the cheese over the bacon.

6. Put back in the oven for about 10 min until the cheese is bubbly and golden.

7. Serve with barbecue sauce.

Chicken Enchilada Bowl

Yields Provided: 4

Nutritional Facts Per Serving:
- 6 g Net Carbs
- 39 g Protein
- 40 g Total Fats
- 569 Calories

Ingredients Needed:
- Coconut oil (2 tbsp.)
- Skinless - boneless chicken thighs (1 lb.)
- Water (.25 cup)
- Red enchilada sauce (.75 cup)
- Chopped onion (.25 cup)
- Diced green chiles (4 oz. can)

Ingredients Needed - Toppings

- Avocado (1 whole - diced)
- Sour cream (.5 cup)
- Shredded cheese (1 cup)
- Chopped pickled jalapenos (.25 cup)
- Roma tomato (1 chopped)
- *Optional*: Serve over plain cauliflower rice or Mexican cauliflower rice

Preparation Steps:

1. Melt the coconut oil in a large pot using the medium heat setting.
2. Sear the chicken until lightly browned.
3. Empty the water and enchilada sauce. Toss in the green chiles and onion.
4. Reduce the temperature and simmer. Prepare the chicken for 17-25 temperature minutes.
5. When the chicken reaches 165° Fahrenheit - internally remove and cool slightly.
6. Shred or chop the meat and toss it back into the pot.
7. Simmer for another ten minutes so the sauce will reduce in volume.
8. To Serve, top with the jalapeno, avocado, tomato, cheese, sour cream, and any other desired toppings.
9. Note: Serve over a portion of cauliflower rice or any

other desired topping making to sure to add any additional carbs used.

Chicken & Green Beans

Yields Provided: 3

Nutritional Facts Per Serving:
- 4 g Net Carbs
- 19 g Protein
- 11 g Total Fats
- 196 Calories

Ingredients Needed:
- Olive oil (2 tbsp.)
- Trimmed green beans (1 cup)
- Whole chicken breasts (2)
- Halved cherry tomatoes (8)
- Italian seasoning (1 tbsp.)
- Salt and pepper (1 tsp.)

Preparation Steps:
1. Warm up a skillet using the medium heat temperature setting. Pour in the oil.
2. Sprinkle the chicken with the pepper, salt, and Italian seasoning.

3. Arrange in the skillet and cook for 10 minutes per side or until well done.

4. Add the tomatoes and beans. Simmer another 5 to 7 minutes and serve.

Chicken Parmesan Meatballs

Yields Provided: 4

Nutritional Facts Per Serving:
- 3.0 g Net Carbs
- 26 g Protein
- 15 g Total Fats
- 257 Calories

Ingredients Needed:
- Three Cheese Garlic Marinara Sauce (.5 cup)
- Ground chicken (1 lb.)
- Minced garlic (3 cloves)
- Grated parmesan cheese (.25 cup)
- Chopped fresh flat-leaf parsley (3 tbsp.)
- Dried Italian seasoning (.5 tsp.)
- Onion powder (.5 tsp.)
- Sea salt (.5 tsp.)
- Black pepper (.25 tsp.)
- Shredded mozzarella cheese (.5 cup)

Preparation Steps:

1. Warm up the oven to 350° Fahrenheit

2. Lightly grease a large baking dish.

3. In a large mixing container, combine 2 tablespoons of the marinara sauce, the ground chicken, parsley, onion powder, garlic, parmesan cheese, Italian seasoning, salt, and pepper

4. Shape the mixture into twelve meatballs.

5. Arrange the prepared meatballs in the baking dish. Leave a small space between each meatball.

6. Bake on the center rack of the oven for 25 minutes.

7. Once it's browned, pull it out of the oven and pour the rest of the sauce over the top of the balls in the pan.

8. Cover the meatballs with mozzarella cheese.

9. Heat up the oven temperature setting to broil.

10. Once it is hot, place the meatballs back to the oven until cheese is melted and golden brown or approximately two to three minutes.

Chicken & Yogurt - Mango Sauce

Yields Provided: 4

Nutritional Facts Per Serving:

- 3.0 g Net Carbs
- 54 g Protein

- 6 g Total Fats
- 296 Calories

Ingredients Needed:

- Chicken breasts (4)
- Plain yogurt (.25 cup)
- Mango (.25 cup)
- Small red onion (1)
- Ground ginger (1 tsp.)
- Freshly cracked black pepper and salt (to your liking)

Preparation Steps:

1. Warm up the oven to 350° Fahrenheit.
2. Dice the chicken, mango, and onion.
3. Fry the chicken in the oil until browned. Toss in the mango and onion. Cook for another three minutes.
4. Stir in the yogurt. Dust with the salt and pepper.
5. Add to a baking dish.
6. Bake for 25 to 30 minutes.
7. Serve when ready.

Enchilada Skillet Dinner

Yields Provided: 4

Nutritional Facts Per Serving:

- 7 g Net Carbs
- 36 g Protein
- 30 g Total Fats
- 455 Calories

Ingredients Needed:
- Small yellow onion (1)
- Ground beef (1.5 lb.)
- Red enchilada sauce (.66 cup)
- Chopped green onions (8)
- Diced Roma tomatoes (2)
- Shredded cheddar cheese (4 oz.)
- *Optional*: Freshly chopped cilantro (as desired)

Preparation Steps:
1. Use a wok or skillet to saute the yellow onion and meat. Drain the juices and add the green onions, tomato, and enchilada sauce.
2. Once it starts to boil, simmer for about 5 minutes. Sprinkle with the salt and cheese. Continue cooking until the cheese has melted.
3. Stir in the cilantro. Serve over chopped lettuce and serving of sour cream. Add the extra carbs and enjoy.

Kung Pao Chicken

Yields Provided: 4

Nutritional Facts Per Serving:

- 4 g Net Carbs
- 23 g Protein
- 18 g Total Fats
- 264 Calories

Ingredients Needed - The Chicken:

- Coconut oil (1 tbsp.)
- Red bell pepper (.33 of 1 medium)
- Celery (2 stalks)
- Peanuts (.25 cup)
- Ground ginger (1 tsp.)
- Minced garlic (.5 tsp.)
- Chicken thighs (4 skinless/boneless)
- *Optional:* Xanthan Gum (.25 tsp.)

Ingredients Needed - The Sauce:

- Liquid aminos (.25 cup)
- Chicken broth (.25 cup)
- Chili garlic sauce/sriracha sauce (1.5 tbsp.)
- Sesame oil (1 tsp.)
- Rice wine vinegar (1 tsp.)
- Liquid stevia (30 drops)

Preparation Steps:

1. Dice the celery stalks and bell pepper into big chunks and set aside.
2. Heat a large skillet using the medium-high heat setting.
3. Chop the chicken thighs into bite-sized chunks.
4. Pour in the coconut oil to the hot skillet and toss in the chunks of chicken.
5. Prepare the sauce while the chicken is cooking. Combine all of the sauce fixings in a mixing container. Whisk well and set to the side for now.
6. Once the chicken is almost fully cooked, fold in the veggies.
7. Simmer for a couple of minutes or until they are slightly tender.
8. Stir in the peanuts and continue to cook for another few minutes while they toast.
9. Add in the ginger and garlic. Stir once more and add in the sauce.
10. Continue cooking and add the xanthan gum to thicken up the sauce even more.
11. Serve with cauliflower rice or on its own.

Lemon Garlic Chicken - Instant Pot

Yields Provided: 6

Nutritional Facts Per Serving:

- 4 g Net Carbs
- 64 g Protein
- 34 g Total Fats
- 582 Calories

Ingredients Needed:

- Boneless chicken thighs skinless or with skin (6-8)
- Sea salt and pepper (as desired)
- Garlic powder (.5 tsp.)
- Olive oil (2 tbsp.)
- Butter (3 tbsp.)
- Onion (.25 cup)
- Garlic cloves (4)
- Italian seasoning (2-4 tsp.)
- Zest of a lemon (.5 of 1)
- Lemon juice (1 lemon)
- Homemade/low sodium chicken broth (.33 cup)
- Chopped fresh parsley and lemon slices for garnish (as desired)
- Heavy cream (2 tbsp.)
- *Also Needed*: Instant Pot OR Cast Iron Skillet

Preparation Steps:

1. Mince or slice the cloves of garlic. Chop the onion.

2. Pour the oil into the Instant Pot.

3. Once it's hot, sauté each side for two to three minutes or until it's browned the way you like it. Depending on the size of your cooker, you might need to work in batches.

4. Once browned, remove from Instant Pot and set aside.

5. Add the butter to the pot to melt.

6. Once hot, just stir in the garlic and onions. Squeeze the lemon and juice over the Instant Pot to deglaze the pan. Sauté for one minute.

7. Stir in the lemon zest, Italian seasoning, and chicken broth.

8. Add the cooked chicken back into the cooker and secure the lid. Close the lid by turning the valve to the sealed position.

9. Adjust the timer for 7 minutes.

10. Once the timer buzzes, natural release the pressure for two minutes. Then, Quick release the remainder of the built up steam and remove the Instant Pot lid.

11. Transfer the chicken from the cooker using tongs to help from being burned by the steam. Set it aside on a large serving container. Pour in the heavy cream (if using) into the cooker.

12. Choose the sauté function.

13. Sauté allowing the sauce to bubble and thicken. Turn it off and add the chicken back to the Instant Pot to coat with sauce.

14. Sprinkle the chicken with chopped parsley and serve hot with your favorite sides.

15. Serve the chicken with cauliflower rice, a salad or spiralized zucchini noodles and a big scoop of the sauce. Add a few lemon slices on the side if desired.

Lemon Parsley Buttered Chicken - Slow Cooked

Yields Provided: 6

Nutritional Facts Per Serving:

- 1 g Net Carbs
- 29 g Protein
- 18 g Total Fats
- 300 Calories

Ingredients Needed:

- Whole roasting chicken (5-6 lb.)
- Black pepper (.25 tsp.)
- Kosher salt (.5 tsp.)
- Water (1 cup)
- Thinly sliced lemon (1)

- Ghee/butter (4 tbsp.)
- Chopped fresh parsley (2 tbsp.)

Preparation Steps:

1. Remove the innards (discard) and rinse the chicken. Dry it off with some paper towels and rub it with the pepper and salt.
2. Arrange the whole chicken in the slow cooker and pour the water into the pot. Set the cooker for 3 hours or when the bird reaches an internal temperature of 165° Fahrenheit at the thickest segment of the thigh.
3. Add the lemon slices, butter, and parsley into the cooker for about ten minutes.
4. *To Serve*: Pour the parsley butter over the chicken and enjoy. Garnish with other toppings of your choosing.

Roasted Chicken & Tomatoes

Yields Provided: 2

Nutritional Facts Per Serving:
- 5 g Net Carbs
- 16 g Protein
- 16 g Total Fats
- 233 Calories

Ingredients Needed:

- Olive oil (1 tbsp.)
- Plum tomatoes (2 quartered)
- Chicken legs – bone-in with skin (2)
- Paprika (1 tsp.)
- Ground oregano (1 tsp.)
- Balsamic vinegar (1 tbsp.)

Preparation Steps:

1. Set the oven temperature setting to 350° Fahrenheit. Grease a roasting pan with a spritz of oil.
2. Rinse and lightly dab the chicken legs dry with a paper towel. Prepare using the oil and vinegar over the skin. Season with the paprika and oregano.
3. Arrange the legs in the pan along with the tomatoes around the edges.
4. Cover with a layer of foil and bake one hour. Baste to prevent the chicken from drying out.
5. Discard the foil and increase the temperature to 425° Fahrenheit.
6. Bake 15 to 30 minutes more until browned and the juices run clear.
7. Serve with a side salad.

Smothered Chicken In Creamy Onion Sauce

Yields Provided:

Nutritional Facts Per Serving: 4

- 3.0 g Net Carbs
- 38 g Protein
- 26 g Total Fats
- 400 Calories

Ingredients Needed:

- Whole green spring onion (1)
- Butter (2 tbsp. or 1-oz.)
- Chicken breast halves (4)
- Sour cream (8 oz.)
- Sea salt (.5 tsp.)

Preparation Steps:

1. Remove all skin and bones from the chicken breasts.
2. Warm up a skillet using the med-high setting to melt the butter.
3. Reduce the setting to med-low and arrange the chicken in the skillet with the butter. Place a lid on the pan and cook about ten minutes.
4. Chop the onion using the white and green sections. Flip the chicken breasts. Cover and simmer another eight or

nine minutes or until done.

5. Combine the onion and cook an additional one or two minutes.

6. Take it off the burner. Blend in the sour cream and salt.

7. Wait for about five minutes. Mix well with your favorite veggies and serve.

Spicy Mexican Lettuce Wraps

Yields Provided: 4

Nutritional Facts Per Serving:

- 5 g Net Carbs
- 16 g Total Fats
- 15 g Protein
- 233 Calories

Ingredients Needed:

- Chicken breasts (2)
- Red pepper (1)
- Hot or mild chili powder (.25 tsp. or to taste)
- Avocado (1)
- Olive oil (2 tbsp.)
- Cheddar cheese (.25 cup)
- Large lettuce leaves (4)
- Medium white onion (1)

- Keto-friendly sour cream - to garnish (1 tbsp.)

Preparation Steps:

1. Dice the pepper, onion, and chicken.
2. Warm up the oil in a skillet on the stovetop. Cook the chicken using the high setting. Stir in the onion, chili powder, and pepper. Simmer 10 to 15 minutes.
3. Slice the avocado and grate the cheese.
4. Portion the mixture into each of the leaves and add a spoon of sour cream.
5. Sprinkle with the pepper and refrigerate until ready to eat.

Stuffed Chicken & Asparagus

Yields Provided: 4
Nutritional Facts Per Serving:

- 2 g Net Carbs
- 32 g Protein
- 25 g Total Fats
- 377 Calories

Ingredients Needed:

- Bacon pieces (.5 lb. or 8 slices)
- Chicken tenders (8 or about 1 lb.)

- Salt (.5 tsp.)
- Black pepper (.25 tsp)
- Asparagus spears (12 or about .5 lb.)

Preparation Steps:

1. Warm up the oven to reach 400° Fahrenheit.
2. Prepare a baking sheet and lay out two slices of bacon.
3. Place the chicken tenders on top of that and sprinkle with a dusting of salt and pepper.
4. Add three spears of the asparagus and wrap with the bacon and chicken to hold it all together.
5. Continue the process and bake for 40 minutes. The bacon should be crispy and the asparagus tender.

Chapter 6: Keto Dinner Options: Pork & Other Meat Favorites

Pork

Pork-Chop Fat Bombs

Yields Provided: 3
Nutritional Facts Per Serving:
- 7 g Net Carbs
- 30 g Protein
- 103 g Total Fats

- 1076 Calories

Ingredients Needed:
- Boneless pork chops (3)
- Oil (.5 cup)
- Medium yellow onion (1)
- Brown mushrooms (8 oz.)
- Nutmeg (1 tsp.)
- Garlic powder (1 tsp.)
- Balsamic vinegar (1 tbsp.)
- Mayonnaise (1 cup)

Preparation Steps:
1. Rinse, drain, and slice the mushrooms. Peel and slice the onion. Put them in a large skillet with the oil and saute until wilted.
2. Place the chops to the side and sprinkle with the nutmeg and garlic powder. Cook until done. Transfer the prepared chops onto a plate.
3. Whisk in the vinegar and mayonnaise into the pan. The thick sauce can be thinned with a bit of chicken broth if needed. (Add 2 tablespoons at a time.)
4. Ladle the sauce over the bomb and serve.

Pork Kebabs

Yields Provided: 4

Nutritional Facts Per Serving:

- 3.3 g Net Carbs
- 34 g Protein
- 9 g Total Fats

Ingredients Needed:

- Hot sauce (2 tsp.)
- Sunflower seed butter (3 tbsp.)
- Minced garlic (1 tbsp.)
- Keto-friendly soy sauce (1 tbsp.)
- Water (1 tbsp.)
- Medium green pepper (1)
- Crushed red pepper (.5 tsp.)
- Squared pork for kebabs (1 lb.)

Preparation Steps:

1. Warm up the oven or grill using the broil or the high heat setting.
2. In a processor or blender, combine the water with the red pepper, soy sauce, garlic, butter, and hot sauce.
3. Slice the pork into squares. Cover with the marinade and rest for one hour.

4. Chop the peppers to fit the skewer. Thread the skewers alternating the pork and peppers.
5. Broil using the high heat setting for five minutes per side.

Stuffed Pork Tenderloin

Yields Provided: 6

Nutritional Facts Per Serving:

- 3.0 g Net Carbs
- 29 g Protein
- 6 g Total Fats
- 194 Calories

Ingredients Needed:

- Pork tenderloin or venison (2 lb.)
- Feta cheese (.5 cup)
- Gorgonzola cheese (.5 cup)
- Onion (1 tsp.)
- Cloves of garlic (2 cloves)
- Crushed almonds (2 tbsp.)
- Sea Salt & black pepper (.5 tsp. each)

Preparation Steps:

1. Warm up the grill. Create a pocket in the tenderloin using a sharp knife.

2. Chop the onion and mince the garlic. Combine the cheeses, onions, almonds, and garlic.

3. Stuff the pork pocket and seal using a skewer.

4. Grill until done with the lid closed (about 300-350° Fahrenheit). The center of the meat should reach 150° Fahrenheit.)

5. Let it rest about 15 minutes tented with foil before serving.

Lamb Options

Garlic & Thyme Lamb Chops

Yields Provided: 6
Nutritional Facts Per Serving:
- 1 g Net Carbs
- 14 g Protein
- 21 g Total Fats
- 252 Calories

Ingredients Needed:
- Lamb chops (6 - 4 oz. each)
- Whole garlic cloves (4)
- Thyme sprigs (2)
- Ground thyme (1 tsp.)

- Olive oil (3 tbsp.)
- Black Pepper and Salt (1 tsp. each)

Preparation Steps:

1. Warm up a skillet using the medium heat setting. Once it's hot, add the olive oil.
2. Season the chops with the spices (pepper, thyme, and salt).
3. Arrange the chops in the skillet along with the garlic and sprigs of thyme.
4. Sauté about 3 to 4 minutes on each side and serve.

Roasted Leg Of Lamb

Yields Provided: 2
Nutritional Facts Per Serving:
- 1 g Net Carbs
- 14 g Total Fats
- 22 g Protein
- 223 Calories

Ingredients Needed:
- Reduced-sodium beef broth (.5 cup)
- Leg of lamb (2 lb.)
- Chopped garlic cloves (6)

- Fresh rosemary leaves (1 tbsp.)
- Back pepper (1 tsp.)
- Salt (2 tsp.)

Preparation Steps:

1. Grease a baking pan and set the oven temperature to 400° Fahrenheit.
2. Arrange the lamb in the pan and add the broth and seasonings.
3. Roast 30 minutes and lower the heat to 350° Fahrenheit. Continue cooking for about one hour or until done.
4. Let the lamb stand about 20 minutes before slicing to serve.
5. Enjoy with some roasted brussels sprouts and extra rosemary for a tasty change of pace.

Other Meat Favorites

Bacon Burger Cabbage Stir Fry

Yields Provided: 10
Nutritional Facts Per Serving:
- 4.5 g Net Carbs
- 32 g Protein

- 22 g Total Fats
- 357 Calories

Ingredients Needed:
- Ground beef (1 lb.)
- Bacon (1 lb.)
- Small onion (1)
- Minced cloves of garlic (3)
- Cabbage (1 lb. - 1 small head)
- Black pepper (.25 tsp.)
- Sea salt (.5 tsp.)

Preparation Steps:
1. Dice the bacon and onion.
2. Combine the beef and bacon in a wok or large skillet. Prepare until done and store in a bowl to keep warm.
3. Mince the onion and garlic. Toss both into the hot grease.
4. Slice and toss in the cabbage and stir-fry until wilted.
5. Blend in the meat and combine. Sprinkle with the pepper and salt as desired.

Bacon Cheeseburger

Yields Provided: 12
Nutritional Facts Per Serving:

- 0.8 g Net Carbs
- 27 g Protein
- 41 g Total Fats
- 489 Calories

Ingredients Needed:

- Low-sodium bacon (16 oz. pkg.)
- Ground beef (3 lb.)
- Eggs (2)
- Medium chopped onion (.5 of 1)
- Shredded cheddar cheese (8 oz.)

Preparation Steps:

1. Fry the bacon and chop to bits. Shred the cheese and dice the onion.
2. Combine the mixture with the beef and blend in the whisked eggs.
3. Prepare 24 burgers and grill them the way you like them. You can make a double-decker since they are small. If you like a larger burger, you can just make 12 burgers as a single-decker.

Cabbage Rolls - Slow Cooked

Yields Provided: 3 rolls each - 5 Servings

Nutritional Facts Per Serving:

- 4 g Net Carbs
- 35 g Protein
- 25 g Total Fats
- 481 Calories

Ingredients Needed:

- Corned beef (3.5 lb.)
- Large savoy cabbage leaves (15)
- White wine (.25 cup)
- Coffee (.25 cup)
- Large lemon (1)
- Medium sliced onion (1)
- Rendered bacon fat (1 tbsp.)
- Erythritol (1 tbsp.)
- Yellow mustard (1 tbsp.)
- Large bay leaf (1)
- Kosher salt (2 tsp.)
- Cloves (.25 tsp.)
- Allspice (.25 tsp.)
- Red pepper flakes (.5 tsp.)
- Whole peppercorns (1 tsp.)
- Mustard seeds (1 tsp.)
- Worcestershire sauce (2 tsp.)

Preparation Steps:

1. Pour the liquids, corned beef, and spices into the cooker. Set the timer for six hours using the low setting.

2. Prepare a pot of boiling water. When the timer on the slow cooker buzzes, add the leaves along with the sliced onion to the water for two to three minutes. Transfer the leaves to a cold-water bath. Blanch them for three to four minutes. Continue boiling the onion.

3. Use a paper towel to dry the leaves. Add the onions and beef.

4. Roll up the cabbage leaves. Drizzle with freshly squeezed lemon juice. Serve any time.

London Broil - Slow Cooked

Yields Provided: 4

Nutritional Facts Per Serving:

- 2.5 g Net Carbs
- 47 g Protein
- 18 g Total Fats
- 409 Calories

Ingredients Needed:

- Minced garlic (2 tsp.)
- London broil (2 lb.)

- Dijon mustard (1 tbsp.)
- Reduced sugar ketchup (2 tbsp.)
- Coconut Aminos/ your choice soy sauce substitute (2 tbsp.)
- Coffee (.5 cup)
- Chicken broth (.5 cup)
- White wine (.25 cup)
- Onion powder (2 tsp.)

Preparation Steps:

1. Arrange the beef in the cooker. Cover both sides with the mustard, soy sauce, ketchup, and minced garlic.
2. Pour the liquids into the cooker and give it a sprinkle of the onion powder.
3. Cook for four to six hours.
4. When the timer buzzes, shred the meat. Combine with the juices and serve.

Nacho Skillet Steak

Yields Provided: 5
Nutritional Facts Per Serving:
- 6 g Net Carbs
- 19 g Protein
- 31 g Total Fats

- 385 Calories

Ingredients Needed:

- Cauliflower (1.5 lb.)
- Turmeric (.5 turmeric)
- Chili powder (1 tsp.)
- Butter (1 tbsp.)
- Beef round tip steak (8 oz.)
- Melted refined coconut oil (.33 cup)
- Shredded cheddar cheese (1 oz.)
- Shredded Monterey Jack cheese (1 oz.)

Ingredients Needed - Optional Garnishes:

- Sour cream (.33 cup)
- Canned - jalapeno slices (1 oz.)
- Avocado (approx. 5 oz.)

Preparation Steps:

1. Warm up the oven temperature to 400° Fahrenheit.
2. Prepare the cauliflower into chip-like shapes.
3. Combine the turmeric, chili powder, and coconut oil in a mixing dish.
4. Toss in the cauliflower and add it to a baking tin. Set the baking timer for 20 to 25 minutes.
5. Over med-high heat in a cast iron skillet, add the

butter. Cook until both sides of the meat is done, flipping just once. Let it rest for 5-10 minutes. Thinly slice and sprinkle with some pepper and salt.

6. When done, transfer the florets to the skillet and add the steak strips. Top it off with the cheese and bake for 5-10 more minutes.
7. Serve with your favorite garnish.
8. Count the carbs for the added garnishes.

Quick & Easy Taco Casserole

Yields Provided: 6
Nutritional Facts Per Serving:
- 6 g Net Carbs
- 45 g Protein
- 18 g Total Fats
- 367 Calories

Ingredients Needed:
- Ground Turkey or Beef (1.5 to 2 lb.)
- Taco seasoning (2 tbsp.)
- Shredded cheddar cheese (8 oz.)
- Salsa (1 cup)
- Cottage cheese (16 oz.)

Preparation Steps:

1. Warm up the oven to reach 400° Fahrenheit.

2. Combine the taco seasoning and ground meat in a casserole dish. Bake for 20 minutes.

3. Combine the salsa and both kinds of cheese. Set aside for now.

4. Carefully transfer the casserole dish from the oven. Drain away the cooking juices from the meat.

5. Break the meat into small pieces and mash with a potato masher or fork.

6. Sprinkle with the cheese. Bake in the oven for 15 to 20 more minutes until the top is browned.

Chapter 7: Keto Appetizers: Side Dishes & Bread

Choices

Bacon Guacamole Fat Bombs

Yields Provided: 6

Nutritional Facts Per Serving:

- 1.5 g Net Carbs
- 15 g Total Fats
- 3.5 g Protein

- 156 Calories

Ingredients Needed:
- Avocado (3.5 oz. or about .5 of 1 large)
- Bacon (about 4 oz. - 4 strips)
- Ghee or butter (.25 cup)
- Crushed cloves of garlic (2)
- Small diced onion (approximately 1.2 oz. or .5 of 1)
- Small finely chopped chili pepper (1)
- Fresh lime juice (1 tbsp. or about .25 of a lime)
- Pinch of ground black pepper or cayenne (1 pinch)
- Salt (to your liking)
- Freshly chopped cilantro (1-2 tbsp.)

Preparation Steps:
1. Heat up the oven temperature to 375° Fahrenheit.
2. Prepare a baking sheet with a layer parchment baking paper.
3. Cook the bacon for 10 to 15 minutes. Save the grease for step four.
4. Peel, deseed, and chop the avocado into a dish along with the garlic, chili pepper, lime juice, cilantro, black pepper, salt, and butter. Use a fork or potato masher to combine the mixture. Blend in the onion.
5. Empty the grease into the bomb fixings, blend well, and

cover for 20 to 30 minutes in the fridge.

6. Break up the bacon into a bowl and roll the six balls in it until coated evenly.

7. Serve or eat when you want a delicious snack.

Bacon Wrapped Mozzarella Sticks

Yields Provided: 2

Nutritional Facts Per Serving:

- 1 g Net Carbs
- 7 g Protein
- 9 g Total Fats
- 103 Calories

Ingredients Needed:

- Thick bacon (2 slices)
- Frigo cheese head mozzarella cheese sticks (1)
- Coconut oil – for frying

Ingredients Needed - Optional Dipping:

- Low-sugar pizza sauce
- Toothpicks

Preparation Steps:

1. Warm up the oil to 350° Fahrenheit in a deep fryer.
2. Slice the cheese stick in half. Wrap it with the bacon and secure it closed using the toothpick.
3. Cook the sticks in the hot fryer for 2-3 minutes.
4. Drain on a towel and cool. Serve with your sauce.

Caramelized Bacon Knots

Yields Provided: 4

Nutritional Facts Per Serving:

- 1 g Net Carbs
- 5 g Protein
- 17 g Total Fats
- 187 Calories

Ingredients Needed:

- Sliced bacon (8)
- Freshly cracked black pepper (1 tbsp.)
- Low carb sweetener of choice (1 tbsp.)

Preparation Steps:

1. Mix equal amounts of the pepper blend and sweetener in a small bowl (ex. erythritol or xylitol would be a good alternative). Set aside.

2. Cut the slices of bacon into half, then tie each half into a knot.

3. Press the bacon knots into the pepper mixture, turning them over to coat as much as possible. Place the dipped knots onto a baking sheet lined with a wire rack.

4. Place the bacon knots under a preheated broiler, and cook for about 5 to 7 minutes on each side, or until cooked to your liking. (You might like to make sure your extractor fan is on as they can make quite a bit of smoke.)

5. Let them cool down, blotting them on paper towels to remove excess grease if necessary.

6. Serve immediately

Cheesy Bacon-Wrapped Hot Dogs

Yields Provided: 6

Nutritional Facts Per Serving:

- 2 g Net Carbs
- 14 g Protein
- 19 g Total Fats
- 283 Calories

Ingredients Needed:

- Bacon slices (12)

- Large beef hot dogs (6)
- Onion (.5 tsp)
- Garlic (.5 tsp)
- Pepper & salt (to your liking)
- Cheddar cheese (2 oz.)

Preparation Steps:

1. Warm up the oven temperature to reach 400° Fahrenheit.
2. Slice each of the hot dogs (not all the way through) and insert the cheese. Wrap the hot dogs with two bacon slices each and secure with a toothpick.
3. Add the seasoning to a dish and roll the dogs through it.
4. Bake 35 to 40 minutes. Serve with your favorite side dishes or as a snack.
5. *Note:* You can adjust the time and cook them as using small chunks for variation.

Coleslaw Stuffed Wraps

Yields Provided: 16 Wraps - 4 Servings
Nutritional Facts Per Serving:
- 3.0 g Net Carbs
- 33 g Protein

- 50 g Total Fats
- 609 Calories

Ingredients Needed:

- Sea salt (.25 tsp.)
- Green onions (.5 cup)
- Red cabbage (3 cups)
- Keto-friendly mayonnaise (.75 cup)
- Apple cider vinegar (2 tsp.)

Ingredients Needed For The Wraps & Other Fillings:

- Ground beef/turkey/pork/chicken– cooked & chilled (1 lb.)
- Collard leaves (16)
- Packed alfalfa sprouts (.33 cup)
- Toothpicks

Preparation Steps:

1. Prepare the meat of choice in a frying pan. Thinly slice the cabbage. Remove the stems from the collards and dice the onions. Add all of the fixings in a large mixing container and stir well.
2. Add a spoonful of the coleslaw on the far edge of the first collard leaf (the side that hasn't been cut). Add the meat and the sprouts.

3. Roll and tuck the sides and insert toothpicks at an angle to hold them together. Continue until all are done. Serve.

Philly Cheesesteak Stuffed Peppers

Yields Provided: 6

Nutritional Facts Per Serving:
- 9 g Net Carbs
- 33 g Protein
- 23 g Total Fats
- 379 Calories

Ingredients Needed - The Onions:
- Olive oil (1 tbsp.)
- Onions (2 large)
- Salt (to taste)

Ingredients Needed - The Peppers:
- Green bell peppers (6 small)
- Olive oil (1 tbsp.)
- Beef top sirloin steak (1 lb.)
- Cauliflower (2 cups)
- Salt
- Provolone cheese (12 oz. sliced)
- *Also Needed:* 9x13 baking pan

Preparation Steps:

1. Thinly slice the steak and remove most of the fat chunks. Slice the onions into ½-inch thickness. Also, discard the membranes and seeds from the peppers and slice into halves. Chop the cauliflower into small florets.

2. In a large skillet, warm up the olive oil using the medium heat setting. It should appear shiny on the surface.

3. Toss in the sliced onions with a pinch of salt.

4. Stir well until the onions are fully covered with the oil.

5. Continue to sauté until they are golden brown and caramelized.

6. Stir every so often for approximately 30 to 45 minutes.

7. Be sure to watch it carefully, especially if your stovetop tends to cook fast. Adjust the heat slowly. Don't stir too often or it will not caramelize properly.

8. Meanwhile, toss the prepared peppers in a large pot and cover with water.

9. Start the timer once it starts boiling. Boil for two to three minutes, until they just begin to soften. Place paper towels on a platter to allow the water to drain from the peppers.

10. Once the peppers have dried out; place them on the baking tin.

11. Warm up the oven to 350° Fahrenheit.

12. Pour the rest of the oil into a large skillet using the medium heat setting. Let the pan get hot before adding the meat.

13. Cook the sliced steak until golden brown, draining out the excess fat. Once it is ready to your liking, place on a platter for now.

14. In a large food processor, add the cauliflower.

15. Pulse until it's similar to regular rice and toss it into the pan that the beef was prepared in. Simmer using the medium heat setting, stirring occasionally until golden brown.

16. Toss in the beef and caramelized onions and sprinkle with sea salt. Stir until well mixed.

17. Stuff the peppers with the mixture. Add a slice of cheese on top of each pepper.

18. Bake for 10 to 15 minutes. The cheese should be melted and the peppers tender.

19. Reset the oven setting to high broil and continue cooking for another two to four minutes until the cheese is golden brown.

Roasted Cauliflower With Blue Cheese Sauce & Bacon

Yields Provided: 4

Nutritional Facts Per Serving:

- 4 g Net Carbs
- 10 g Protein
- 32 g Total Fats
- 352 Calories

Ingredients Needed:

- Cauliflower (1 head)
- Mayonnaise (.5 cup)
- Bacon crumbs (.5 cup)
- Blue cheese chunks (1 cup)

Preparation Steps:

1. Quarter the cauliflower and remove the stem and leaves.
2. Finely chop the blue cheese.
3. Preheat oven to 350° Fahrenheit.
4. Spritz a baking tin with a misting of cooking oil spray. Arrange the cauliflower quarters on the baking pan. Roast for 30 minutes.
5. Meanwhile, make the sauce by combining the blue cheese and mayonnaise.
6. After 30 minutes the cauliflower should be slightly tender.
7. Finish up by dressing the cauliflower with the blue cheese sauce.

8. Drizzle with the bacon bits.

9. Bake until the cheese sauce is golden or for 10 to 15 minutes.

Side Dishes

Asparagus & Tofu Mash

Yields Provided: 1

Nutritional Facts Per Serving:
- 8 g Net Carbs
- 20 g Protein
- 57 g Total Fats
- 601 Calories

Ingredients Needed:
- Asparagus (.5 cup)
- Spring onions (1 tbsp.)
- Coconut cream (4 tbsp.)
- Parsley (.5 tbsp.)
- Lemon juice (1 tsp.)
- Silky tofu (1 cup)
- Coconut oil (2 tbsp.)

Preparation Steps:

1. Chop the spring onion, asparagus, and tofu.

2. Prepare the cubed tofu in a steamer unit for 8-10 minutes.

3. Fill a pot of water and wait for it to boil. Toss in the asparagus for about two minutes to blanch and drain.

4. Use medium heat on the stovetop and add the oil to saute the onions i.

5. Toss all of the fixings into a blender and mix until creamy smooth.

   Serve piping hot.

Baked Marinara Spaghetti Squash

Yields Provided: 4

Nutritional Facts Per Serving:

- 5 g Net Carbs
- 6 g Total Fats
- 3 g Protein
- 92 Calories

Ingredients Needed:

- Marinara sauce – no sugar (.5 cup)
- Spaghetti squash (1)
- Sliced mushrooms (.5 cup)
- Black Pepper & Salt (1 tsp. each)

- Olive oil (1 tbsp.)
- Shredded mozzarella cheese (.25 cup)

Preparation Steps:

1. Program the oven setting to 375 °Fahrenheit.
2. Cut the squash in half and discard the seeds.
3. Drizzle with the oil and sprinkle with the pepper and salt.
4. Flip onto the baking tin with the cut side down.
5. Bake 35 minutes until the squash is removed with a fork easily. If it's not done, cook another 10 minutes.
6. Serve.

Caprese Skewers

Yields Provided: 2
Nutritional Facts Per Serving:

- 7 g Net Carbs
- 25 g Protein
- 27 g Total Fats
- 384 Calories

Ingredients Needed:

- Baby mozzarella cheese balls (2 cups)
- Cherry or baby heirloom tomatoes (2 cups)

- Pitted mixed olives (.5 cup)
- Green/red pesto (2 tbsp.)
- Fresh basil (2 tbsp.)

Preparation Steps:

1. Rinse the basil and tomatoes.
2. Marinate the kalamata and green olives in extra-virgin olive oil with the oregano.
3. Combine the mozzarella with the pesto.
4. Arrange the olives, mozzarella, and tomatoes onto the skewers and garnish with the basil.
5. Serve any time.

Cauliflower Mac & Cheese

Yields Provided: 4

Nutritional Facts Per Serving:

- 7 g Net Carbs
- 11 g Protein
- 23 g Total Fats
- 294 Calories

Ingredients Needed:

- Cauliflower (1 head)
- Butter (3 tbsp.)

- Unsweetened almond milk (.25 cup)
- Heavy cream (.25 cup)
- Cheddar cheese (1 cup)
- Freshly cracked black pepper & Sea salt (to your liking)

Preparation Steps:

1. Use a sharp knife to slice the cauliflower into small florets. Shred the cheese.
2. Prepare the oven to reach 450° Fahrenheit.
3. Cover a baking tray with a layer of parchment baking paper or foil.
4. Add 2 tbsp. of the butter to a pan and melt. Add the florets and butter together. Sprinkle with the pepper and salt. Place the cauliflower on the baking pan and roast 10 to 15 minutes.
5. Warm up the rest of the butter, milk, heavy cream, and cheese in the microwave or double boiler. Pour the cheese over the cauliflower and serve.

Cauliflower Soufflé

Yields Provided: 6

Nutritional Facts Per Serving:
- 5 g Net Carbs
- 17 g Protein
- 28 g Total Fats

- 342 Calories

Ingredients Needed:

- Eggs (2)
- Cauliflower (1 head)
- Asiago cheese (.5 cup)
- Sour cream/Yogurt (.5 cup)
- Cream (2 tbsp.)
- Cream cheese (2 oz.)
- Mild/sharp cheddar cheese (1 cup)
- Softened butter or ghee (2 tsp.)
- Chives (.25 cup)
- *Optional*: Crumbled cooked bacon (6 slices)

Preparation Steps:

1. In a food processor, combine the two kinds of cheese, sour cream, cream cheese, cream, and eggs. Pulse until smooth and frothy.

2. Chop the cauliflower and add to the mixture (pulse 2 seconds at a time). Blend in the butter and chives. Empty into a 1 ¼-quart casserole dish.

3. Pour the water into the Instant Pot. Secure the top and cook for 12 minutes using the high-pressure setting. Natural release for ten minutes, and quick release.

4. Garnish with the bacon if you choose.

Cauliflower Spinach Bowl

Yields Provided: 1

Nutritional Facts Per Serving:

- 7 g Net Carbs
- 17 g Protein
- 45 g Total Fats
- 499 Calories

Ingredients Needed:

- Cauliflower (.75 cups)
- Spinach (1 cup)
- Almonds (.25 cup)
- Garlic (.25 tbsp.)
- Cilantro (.5 cup)
- Sunflower seeds (.5 tbsp.)
- Olive oil (2 tbsp.)
- Ricotta cheese (.5 tbsp.)

Preparation Steps:

1. Chop the cauliflower, garlic, and onions.
2. Warm up the oven to 375° Fahrenheit.
3. Add the almonds on a baking tin to roast for 7-10 minutes. Let it cool.
4. Use a food processor and add the cauliflower. Pulse

until it's rice-like.

5. In another skillet, warm up one tablespoon of oil using the medium heat setting. Toss in the riced cauliflower and chopped garlic. Saute until golden brown and sprinkle with the pepper and salt.

   Toss in the cilantro and spinach, but don't stir. Let them wilt on top for two to three minutes.

6. Garnish with the sunflower seeds, almonds, and ricotta before serving.

Cheesy Kale Casserole

Yields Provided: 8

Nutritional Facts Per Serving:

- 1 g Net Carbs
- 11 g Protein
- 14 g Total Fats
- 195 Calories

Ingredients Needed:

- Eggs (6)
- Chopped kale (2.5 cups)
- Chopped onion (1)
- Shredded cheddar cheese (1 cup)
- Heavy cream (.5 cup)

- Herbs de Provence (1 tsp.)
- Pepper & Salt (as desired)
- Water (1 cup)

Preparation Steps:

1. Measure and pour the water into the Instant Pot. Add the trivet.
2. Whisk the eggs, salt, cream, and pepper.
3. Mix in the onion, kale, cheese, and Herbs de Provence.
4. Pour the fixings into a pan that will fit on the rack of the Instant Pot. Arrange on the trivet and secure the top.
5. Use the high-pressure setting and cook for 20 minutes.
6. Natural release the pressure (10 min. approx.) and serve.

Creamy Green Cabbage

Yields Provided: 4

Nutritional Facts Per Serving:

- 8 g Net Carbs
- 4 g Protein
- 42 g Total Fats
- 432 Calories

Ingredients Needed:

- Butter (2 oz.)
- Shredded green cabbage (1.5 lb.)
- Coconut cream (1.25 cups)
- Finely chopped fresh parsley (8 tbsp.)
- Pepper & Salt (to your liking)

Preparation Steps:

1. Shred the cabbage and add to a skillet with the butter. Saute until golden brown.
2. Stir in the cream with a sprinkle of salt and pepper. Simmer.
3. Garnish with the parsley and serve while warm.

Edamame Kelp Noodles

Yields Provided: 2
Nutritional Facts Per Serving:

- 5 g Net Carbs
- 8 g Protein
- 9 g Total Fats
- 139 Calories

Ingredients Needed:

- Kelp noodles (1 pkg.)

- Shelled edamame (.5 cup)
- Julienned carrots (.25 cup)
- Sliced mushrooms (.25 cup)
- Frozen spinach (1 cup)

Ingredients Needed - The Sauce:

- Sesame oil (1 tbsp.)
- Tamari (2 tbsp.)
- Ground ginger (.5 tsp.)
- Garlic powder (.5 tsp.)
- Sriracha (.25 tsp.)

Preparation Steps:

1. Soak the noodles in water. Drain well.
2. Use the medium heat setting and place the sauce fixings in a saucepan. Add the veggies and warm.
3. Stir in the noodles and simmer for two to three minutes, stirring occasionally.

Garlic Zucchini – Slow Cooked

Yields Provided: 6

Nutritional Facts Per Serving:

- 1 g Net Carbs
- 1 g Protein

- 10 g Total Fats
- 93 Calories

Ingredients Needed:
- Olive oil (4 tbsp.)
- Cloves of garlic (3)
- Chopped onion (1)
- Zucchini (3 Medium)
- Paprika – 1 dash
- Pepper & Salt (as desired)

Preparation Steps:
1. Thinly slice the zucchini and mince the garlic.
2. Combine all of the components into the Instant Pot. Stir and close the top securely.
3. Select the slow-cook function and adjust the timer for 4 hours.
4. About halfway through (2 hrs.), open the lid and stir, brown the other side and secure the top once again.
5. After 4 hours total, natural release the pressure and serve.

Mexican Cauli-Rice

Yields Provided: 4

Nutritional Facts Per Serving:

- 5 g Net Carbs
- 4 g Protein
- 8 g Total Fats
- 121 Calories

Ingredients Needed:

- White onion (.5 of 1 medium)
- Clove of garlic (1)
- Olive oil (2 tbsp.)
- Cumin (1 tsp.)
- Chili powder (1 tbsp.)
- Cauliflower (1 lb. - riced)
- Diced tomatoes – no salt (1 can - 14.5 oz.)
- Pink Himalayan salt/sea salt (to your liking)

Ingredients Needed - Possible Garnishes:

- Sliced avocado
- Limes
- Minced cilantro
- Sliced jalapeno
- Sour cream
- Extra-virgin olive oil

Preparation Steps:

1. Use the medium temperature setting on the stovetop and pour in the oil.

2. Dice the garlic and onion and toss into the pan. Sauté for two to three minutes. When they are soft, add the spices and continue sauteing for 30 seconds or so.

3. Toss in the riced cauliflower and saute for another five to seven minutes until it is starting to get crispy around the edges. It will look similar to fluffed rice.

4. Add salt if you wish, and serve.

5. You can keep it in the fridge for about four days. Have it for some leftovers.

Mushroom & Cauliflower Risotto

Yields Provided: 4

Nutritional Facts Per Serving:

- 4 g Net Carbs
- 17 g Total Fats
- 1 g Protein
- 186 Calories

Ingredients Needed:

- Grated head of cauliflower (1)

- Vegetable stock (1 cup)
- Chopped mushrooms (9 oz.)
- Butter (2 tbsp.)
- Coconut cream (1 cup)
- Pepper and Salt (to taste)

Preparation Steps:

1. Pour the stock in a saucepan. Boil and set aside.
2. Prepare a skillet with butter and saute the mushrooms until golden.
3. Grate and stir in the cauliflower and stock.
4. Simmer and add the cream, cooking until the cauliflower is al dente. Serve.

Parmesan Onion Rings

Yields Provided: 4

Nutritional Facts Per Serving:
- 5 g Net Carbs
- 7 g Total Fats
- 3 g Protein
- 89 Calories

Ingredients Needed:
- Olive oil (as needed for frying)

- Large white onion (1)
- Medium egg (1)
- Pepper (as desired)
- Coconut flour (1 tbsp.)
- Parmesan cheese (1 tbsp.)
- Heavy cream (1 tbsp.)

Preparation Steps:

1. In a skillet, warm the oil until it reaches 350° Fahrenheit.
2. Slice the onions into thick rings.
3. Whisk the flour, cheese, and pepper.
4. Whisk the cream and egg together.
5. Dip the sliced rings into the wet and then the dry mixture. Gently add to the oil. Cook for two to three minutes. Drain on a towel-lined platter. Serve while hot.

Red Pepper Zoodles

Yields Provided: 4

Nutritional Facts Per Serving:

- 4 g Net Carbs
- 17 g Total Fats
- 5 g Protein

- 198 Calories

Ingredients Needed:
- Garlic (1 clove)
- Red bell peppers (1)
- Almond milk (1 cup)
- Olive oil (1 tbsp.)
- Almond butter (.25 cup)
- Salt (1 tsp.)

Steps for Preparation:
1. Use a layer of aluminum foil to cover a baking sheet.
2. Add the bell peppers to the baking sheet before placing them on the top level of your broiler and letting them cook until blackened. Remove and cool.
3. Once they have cooled you can remove the skins, stems, seeds, and ribs.
4. Add the prepared mixture, along with the remaining sauce ingredients, and blend thoroughly. Season as desired.
5. Serve with zoodles as well as a variety of potential toppings including things like truffle oil, goat cheese, or parsley.

Roasted Veggies

Yields Provided: 6

Nutritional Facts Per Serving:

- 3.0 g Net Carbs
- 2 g Protein
- 5 g Total Fats
- 65 Calories

Ingredients Needed:

- Button mushrooms (1 cup)
- Sliced zucchini (2)
- Large grape tomatoes (8)
- Chopped asparagus spears (10)
- Chopped yellow pepper (1)
- Olive oil (2 tbsp.)
- Lemon juice (1 tbsp.)
- Salt (.5 tsp.)

Preparation Steps:

1. Prepare the oven to 450° Fahrenheit. Lightly grease a baking pan.
2. Slice and chop the veggies. Place them into the prepared pan.
3. Squeeze the lemon for the juice and toss the veggies

with the mixture of oil and fresh juice.

4. Sprinkle with the salt and roast 40 minutes.

Bread Choices

Bread Twists

Yields Provided: 10
Nutritional Facts Per Serving:

- 1 g Net Carbs
- 7 g Protein
- 18 g Total Fats
- 204 Calories

Ingredients Needed:

- Almond flour (.5 cup)
- Coconut flour (4 tbsp.)
- Salt (.5 tsp.)
- Baking powder (1 tsp.)
- Shredded cheese - your choice (1.5 cups)
- Butter (2.33 oz.)
- Egg (2 - Use 1 for brushing the tops)
- Green pesto (2 oz.)

Preparation Steps:

1. Warm up the oven to reach 350° Fahrenheit.

2. Prepare a cookie sheet with a layer of parchment paper.

3. Mix all of the dry fixings.

4. Use the low heat setting to melt the butter and cheese together. Stir until smooth and add the egg. Stir well.

5. Combine all of the fixings to make the dough.

6. Roll out the dough between 2 layers of parchment paper until it is about one inch thick. Remove the top sheet.

7. Spread the pesto on top of the dough and slice into one-inch strips.

8. Twist the dough and arrange on the baking tin. Brush the twists with the second egg (gently whisked).

9. Bake until golden brown or about 15 to 20 minutes.

Chapter 8: Keto Desserts & Smoothies

Desserts

Almond Blackberry Chia Pudding

Yields Provided: 2

Nutritional Facts Per Serving:

- 1 g Net Carbs
- 8 g Total Fats
- 2 g Protein
- 109 Calories

Ingredients Needed:

- Chia seeds (.25 cup)
- Raw honey (drizzle)
- Sliced almonds (2-3 tbsp.)
- Vanilla almond milk (1.5 cups)
- Fresh blackberries (6 oz.)

Preparation Steps:

1. Rinse and add the berries into a dish. Crush with a fork until creamy.
2. Pour in the raw honey, milk, and chia seeds. Stir well.
3. Refrigerate for several hours or overnight for the most delicious results.
4. Sprinkle with the almonds and several blackberries.
5. Serve any time.

Almond Creamy & Dark Chocolate Bombs

Yields Provided: 12

Nutritional Facts Per Serving:

- 7 g Total Fats
- 2 g Net Carbs
- 2 g Protein
- 86 Calories

Ingredients Needed:

- Regular cream cheese (1 oz.)
- Coconut butter - not oil (4 tbsp.)
- Almond butter (4 tbsp.)
- 73% organic super dark chocolate (2 sections)
- Sugar-free French vanilla syrup (2 tbsp.)
- Unsweetened cocoa powder (1 tbsp.)
- *Optional:* Stevia/sweetener of choice (2 packs)

Preparation Steps:

1. In a microwavable dish, add all fixings except the coconut butter.
2. Cook at 15-second intervals until the chocolate has melted. Stir all ingredients until incorporated.
3. Spoon the batter into 12 muffin tins or use silicone candy molds.
4. Place the container of bombs in the freezer for about one hour.
5. Just quickly pop them out using a butter knife. Store and enjoy anytime you want a delicious snack!

Chocolate Chip Cookie Dough Fat Bomb

Yields Provided: 20

Nutritional Facts Per Serving:

- 2 g Net Carbs
- 14 g Total Fat
- 2 g Protein
- 139 Calories

Ingredients Needed:

- Cream cheese (1 pkg. - 8 oz.)
- Salted butter (.5 cup or 1 stick)
- Sweetener – swerve/erythritol (.33 cup)
- Almond butter or creamy peanut butter - only salt and peanuts (.5 cup)
- Vanilla extract (1 tsp.)
- Baking chips - stevia sweetened chocolate chips (4 oz.)

Preparation Steps:

1. Remove the cream cheese from the fridge for about 20 to 30 minutes to soften.
2. Use a mixer to blend all of the fixings. Refrigerate at least 30 minutes before adding them onto a tray lined with a layer of parchment paper.
3. Spray an ice cream scoop with a spritz of cooking spray (preferably coconut oil).
4. Scoop out 20 bomb portions and place them onto the prepared pan.
5. Freeze for a minimum of 30 minutes.

6. Store in the fridge in a zipper-type plastic bag for convenience.

Chocolate Mousse

Yields Provided: 2

Nutritional Facts Per Serving:
- 4 g Net Carbs
- 4 g Protein
- 50 g Total Fats
- 460 Calories

Ingredients Needed:
- Butter (4 tbsp.)
- Cream Cheese (4 tbsp.)
- Heavy whipping cream (1.5 tbsp.)
- Swerve or another natural sweetener (1 tbsp.)
- Unsweetened cocoa powder (1 tbsp.)

Preparation Steps:
1. Remove the butter and cream cheese from the fridge about 30 minutes before time to prepare to become room temperature.
2. Chill a bowl and whisk the cream. Place back in the refrigerator for now.

3. Use a hand mixer to combine the sweetener, cream cheese, cocoa powder, and butter until well mixed.

4. Remove the refrigerated cream and fold into the chocolate mixture using a rubber scraper.

5. Portion into two dessert bowls and chill for one hour.

Chocolate Muffins - Instant Pot

Yields Provided: 6

Nutritional Facts Per Serving:

- 5 g Net Carbs
- 14 g Total Fats
- 7 g Protein
- 193 Calories

Ingredients Needed:

- Flaxseed Meal (1 cup)
- Sweetened cocoa powder (.25 cup)
- Pumpkin puree (.5 cup)
- Melted coconut oil (2 g Protein
- 8 g Total Fats
- 89 Calories

Ingredients Needed:

- Coconut oil (.5 cup)

- Peanut butter (.5 cup)
- Liquid stevia granulated sweetener (to your liking)
- *Also Needed*: 12-18 count muffin tin & liners or a loaf pan

Preparation Steps:
1. Prepare the tin of choice with a spritz of oil.
2. Combine the oil and peanut butter together on the stovetop or microwave. Melt and add the sweetener.
3. Scoop into the tins or loaf pan and freeze.
4. You can serve with a drizzle of melted chocolate – but remember to count the carbs.

Peanut Butter Protein Bars

Yields Provided: 12
Nutritional Facts Per Serving:
- 3.0 g Net Carbs
- 7 g Protein
- 14 g Total Fats
- 172 Calories

Ingredients Needed:
- Almond meal (1.5 cups)
- Keto-friendly chunky peanut butter (1 cup)

- Egg whites (2)
- Almonds (.5 cup)
- Cashews (.5 cup)
- *Also Needed*: Baking pan

Preparation Steps:

1. Heat the oven ahead of time to reach 350° Fahrenheit.
2. Spritz a baking dish lightly with coconut or olive oil.
3. Combine all of the fixings and add to the prepared dish.
4. Bake for 15 minutes and cut into 12 pieces once they're cooled.
5. Store in the refrigerator to keep them fresh.

Pumpkin Bars With Cream Cheese Frosting

Yields Provided: 16

Nutritional Facts Per Serving:

- 2 g Net Carbs
- 3 g Protein
- 13 g Total Fats
- 139 Calories

Ingredients Needed:

- Large eggs (2)
- Coconut oil (.25 cup)

- Cream cheese (2 oz.)
- Pumpkin puree (1 cup)
- Almond flour (1 cup)
- Vanilla extract (1 tsp.)
- Gluten-free baking powder (2 tsp.)
- Erythritol sweetener blend (.66 cups
- Pumpkin pie spice (1 tsp.)
- Sea salt (.5 tsp.)

Ingredients Needed - The Frosting:

- Powdered erythritol (.5 cup)
- *Optional*: Heavy cream (1 tbsp.)
- Softened cream cheese (6 oz.)
- Vanilla extract (1 tsp.)
- Also Needed: 9 x 9 baking pan

Preparation Steps:

1. Warm up the oven until it reaches 350° Fahrenheit. Cover the baking pan with parchment paper.
2. In a double boiler or microwave, melt the coconut oil and cream cheese.
3. Combine the vanilla, eggs, cream cheese mixture, and puree using a hand mixer until smooth using the medium-speed setting.
4. Whisk the dry fixings (salt, pie spice, baking powder,

sweetener, and flour).

5. Mix all the ingredients with the mixer until just combined and pour into the pan.

6. Bake for 20-30 minutes. Cool completely.

7. Prepare the frosting with each of the ingredients when the bars are cooled. If it's too thick, just add a little cream or milk.

8. Slice into 16 equal portions. Enjoy.

Pumpkin Bread

Yields Provided: 8

Nutritional Facts Per Serving:

- 5 g Net Carbs
- 8 g Protein
- 26g Total Fats
- 311 Calories

Ingredients Needed:

- Almond flour (1 cup)
- Libby's Canned Pumpkin (1 small can)
- Baking powder (.5 tsp.)
- Coconut flour (.5 cup)
- Heavy cream (.5 cup)
- Stevia (.5 cup)

- Melted butter (1 stick)
- Large eggs (4)
- Vanilla (1.5 tsp.)
- Pumpkin spice (2 tsp.)

Preparation Steps:

1. Set the oven temperature setting to 350° Fahrenheit. Grease a pie plate with a spritz of coconut oil.
2. Combine all of the fixings in a mixing container until light and fluffy.
3. Pour the batter into the prepared pan. Bake for approximately 70 to 90 minutes.

Shamrock Shake

Yields Provided: 1
Nutritional Facts Per Serving:
- 5 g Net Carbs
- 25 g Protein
- 25 g Total Fats
- 352 Calories

Ingredients Needed:
- Loosely packed spinach or less- to taste (2 cups)
- Loosely packed fresh mint leaves (.25 cup)

- Vanilla protein powder of choice ex.Vega Sport (.25 cup)
- Mashed avocado OR full-fat canned coconut milk (.5 cup)
- Nondairy milk of choice (1 cup) OR Ice cubes (2 cups for a thicker drink)

Preparation Steps:

1. Prepare a high-speed blender with all of the fixings.
2. Pulse until creamy smooth.

Strawberries With Coconut Whip

Yields Provided: 4

Nutritional Facts Per Serving:

- 10 g Net Carbs
- 4 g Protein
- 31 g Total Fats
- 342 Calories

Ingredients Needed:

- Strawberries or other favorite berries (4 cups)
- Refrigerated coconut cream (2 cans)
- 70% or darker unsweetened chopped dark chocolate (1 oz.)

Preparation Steps:

1. Remove the solidified cream from the can of milk and set aside for another time; saving the liquid. Pour it into a mixing container and whip with a hand mixer until it forms stiff peaks (approximately five minutes).

2. Slice the berries and portion into four dishes. Serve with a dollop of the cream. Garnish with the chopped chocolate and a few berries. Serve.

Strawberry Cheesecake Fat Bombs

Yields Provided: 12
Nutritional Facts Per Serving:

- .85 g Net Carbs
- 1 g Protein
- 7 g Total Fats
- 67 Calories

Ingredients Needed:

- Coconut oil or softened butter (.25 cup)
- Softened cream cheese (.75 cup)
- Fresh/frozen strawberries (.5 cup)
- Liquid stevia (10-15 drops) or powdered erythritol (2 tbsp.)
- Vanilla extract (1 tbsp.)

Preparation Steps:

1. Mix the butter or coconut oil with the cream cheese in a mixing container. Let it rest 30 to 60 minutes until it is room temperature. (Don't microwave.)

2. Prepare the berries and remove the stems. Add them to a dish and mash until smooth. Stir in the stevia and vanilla. Mix well using a food processor or hand whisk.

3. Scoop out the mixture and add into candy molds or muffin silicone molds.

4. Let the bombs rest in the freezer until set; usually about two hours.

5. Just pop them out and enjoy. Store in the freezer.

Strawberry Thumbprint Delights

Yields Provided: 16
Nutritional Facts Per Serving:

- 1 g Net Carbs
- 2 g Protein
- 9 g Total Fats
- 95 Calories

Ingredients Needed:

- Almond flour (1 cup)
- Baking powder (.5 tsp.)

- Coconut flour (2 tbsp.)
- Sugar-free strawberry jam (2 tbsp.)
- Shredded coconut (1 tbsp.)
- Eggs (2)
- Erythritol (.5 cup)
- Coconut oil (4 tbsp.)
- Salt (.5 tsp.)
- Cinnamon (.5 tsp.)
- Almond extract (.5 tsp.)
- Vanilla extract (.5 tsp.)

Preparation Steps:

1. Warm up the oven temperature to 350° Fahrenheit. Cover a cookie tin with a sheet of parchment paper.

2. Whisk the dry fixings and make a hole in the middle. Fold in the wet fixings to form a dough. Break it into 16 segments and roll into balls.

3. Arrange each one on the prepared cookie sheet and bake 15 minutes.

4. When done, cool completely and add a dab of jam to each one with a sprinkle of coconut.

Streusel Scones

Yields Provided: 12

Nutritional Facts Per Serving:

- 3.5 g Net Carbs
- 0.6 g Protein
- 12 g Total Fats
- 145 Calories

Ingredients Needed:

- Baking powder (1 tsp.)
- Almond flour (2 cups)
- Ground stevia leaf (.25 tsp.)
- Fresh blueberries (1 cup)
- Egg (1)
- Salt (1 pinch)
- Almond milk (2 tbsp.)

Ingredients Needed - The Topping:

- Egg white (1 tbsp.)
- Ground cinnamon (.5 tsp.)
- Slivered almonds (.25 cup.)
- Stevia (1 pinch)

Preparation Steps:

1. Prepare the topping and set it aside.

2. Warm up the oven to 375° Fahrenheit.

3. Sift the baking powder, salt, flour, and stevia. Blend in the blueberries.

4. In another container, whisk the egg and milk until combined. Fold into the dry fixings and shape into 12 scones.

5. Arrange each of the scones on a parchment paper-lined baking tin.

6. Bake until golden brown or 20 to 22 minutes.

7. Add the prepared toppings serve.

Stuffed Pecan Fat Bombs

Yields Provided: 1

Nutritional Facts Per Serving:

- 2 g Net Carbs
- 11 g Protein
- 31 g Total Fats
- 150 Calories

Ingredients Needed:

- Pecan halves (4)
- Coconut butter/unsalted butter (.5 tbsp.)

- Cream cheese (1 oz.)
- Your favorite flavor mix – herb or veggie
- Sea salt (1 pinch)

Preparation Steps:

1. Warm up the oven to 350° Fahrenheit. Once it's hot, toast the pecans for 8 to 10 minutes and cool.
2. Let the cream cheese and butter soften. Add the mixture with your favorite flavored mix, veggie, or herbs. Mix until smooth.
3. Spread the tasty fixings between the two pecan halves.
4. Drizzle with some sea salt and serve.

Walnut Orange Chocolate Bombs

Yields Provided: 8

Nutritional Facts Per Serving:

- 2 g Net Carbs
- 2 g Protein
- 9 g Total Fats
- 87 Calories

Ingredients Needed:

- 85% Cocoa dark chocolate (12.5 grams)
- Extra-Virgin coconut oil (.25 cup)

- Orange peel or orange extract (.5 tbsp.)
- Walnuts (1.75 cups chopped)
- Cinnamon (1 tsp.)
- Stevia (10-15 drops)

Preparation Steps:

1. Melt the chocolate in a saucepan or the microwave. Add cinnamon and coconut oil. Sweeten mixture with stevia.
2. Pour in the fresh orange peel and chopped walnuts.
3. In a muffin tin or in candy mold, spoon in the mixture.
4. Place in the refrigerator for one to three hours until the mixture is solid.

White Chocolate Fat Bombs

Yields Provided: 8
Nutritional Facts Per Serving:
- 0.3 g Net Carbs
- 0.9 g Protein
- 20 g Total Fats
- 265 Calories

Ingredients Needed:
- Coconut oil (4 tbsp.)

- Erythritol (4 tbsp. powdered)
- Butter (4 tbsp.)
- Cocoa butter (4 oz.)
- Chopped walnuts (.5 cup)
- Vanilla extract (.5 tsp.)
- Salt (.25 tsp)

Preparation Steps:

1. Prepare a pan using the medium-high temperature setting on the stovetop. Add the butter, coconut oil, and cocoa butter.
2. Once it's melted, add the walnuts, salt, stevia, vanilla extract, and erythritol. Mix well.
3. Pour into the silicone mold. Store the treats in the refrigerator for one hour before serving.

Smoothies

Almond Milk & Avocado Smoothie

Yields Provided: 1
Nutritional Facts Per Serving:
- 4 g Net Carbs
- 6 g Protein
- 58 g Total Fats
- 587 Calories

Ingredients Needed:

- Avocado (1)
- Ice cubes (6)
- EZ-Sweetz sweetener (6 drops)
- Unsweetened almond milk (3 oz.)
- Coconut cream (3 oz.)

Preparation Steps:

1. Slice the avocado lengthwise before removing the seeds and the skin.
2. Toss the avocado with the rest of the fixings into the blender.
3. Toss in the ice cubes and blend until the smoothie is creamy smooth.

Blueberry Essence

Yields Provided: 1

Nutritional Facts Per Serving:

- 3.0 g Net Carbs
- 31 g Protein
- 21 g Total Fats
- 343 Calories

Ingredients Needed:

- Coconut milk (1 cup)
- Blueberries (.25 cup)
- Vanilla Essence (1 tsp.)
- MCT oil (1 tsp.)
- Ice cubes (2-3)

Preparation Steps:

1. For a quick burst of energy, combine each of the fixings in a blender.
2. Puree until it reaches the desired consistency.
3. Pour and serve into a chilled glass.

Cinnamon Smoothie

Yields Provided: 1

Nutritional Facts Per Serving:

- 5 g Net Carbs
- 24 g Protein
- 40 g Total Fats
- 467 Calories

Ingredients Needed:

- Cinnamon (.5 tsp.)
- Coconut milk (.5 cup)

- Water (.5 cup)
- Extra-Virgin coconut oil/MCT oil (1 tbsp.)
- Ground chia seeds (1 tbsp.)
- Plain or vanilla whey protein (.25 cup)
- Stevia drops - optional (as desired)

Preparation Steps:

1. Pour the milk, cinnamon, protein powder, and chia seeds in a blender.
2. Empty the coconut oil, ice, and water.
3. Add a few drops of stevia if desired.

5-Minute Mocha Smoothie

Yields Provided: 3
Nutritional Facts Per Serving:

- 4 g Net Carbs
- 3 g Protein
- 16 g Total Fats
- 176 Calories

Ingredients Needed:

- Avocado (1)
- Coconut milk – from the can (.5 cup)
- Unsweetened almond milk (1.5 cups)

- Instant coffee crystals – regular or decaffeinated (2 tsp.)
- Vanilla extract (1 tsp.)
- Erythritol blend/granulated stevia (3 tbsp.)
- Unsweetened cocoa powder (3 tbsp.)

Preparation Steps:

1. Slice the avocado in half. Discard the pit and remove most of the center. Add it along with the rest of the fixings into a blender.
2. Mix until it's like you like it. Serve in three chilled glasses.

Spinach & Cucumber Smoothies

Yields Provided: 2

Nutritional Facts Per Serving:
- 3.0 g Net Carbs
- 10 g Protein
- 32 g Total Fats
- 330 Calorie

Ingredients Needed:

- Ice cubes (6)
- Your choice of sweetener (to taste)

- Coconut milk (.75 cup)
- MCT oil (2 tbsp.)
- Cucumber (2.5 oz.)
- Spinach (2 handfuls)
- Coconut milk (1 cup)
- Xanthan gum (.25 tsp.)

Preparation Steps:

1. Cream the coconut milk: This is a simple process. All you need to do is put the can of coconut milk in the fridge overnight. The next morning, open the can and spoon out the coconut milk that has solidified. Don't shake the can before opening. Discard the liquids.

2. Add all of the ingredients, save the ice cubes, to the blender and blend using the low speed until pureed. Thin with water as needed.

3. Add in the ice cubes and blend until the smoothie reaches your desired consistency.

Chapter 9: 30-Day Ketogenic Meal Plan

Each of these recipes has the net carbs per serving posted. You will see how flexible the plan is when you look at how easy it is to use just the recipes in this cookbook for 30 full days including three meals, snacks, and desserts.

The meals are planned so you still have flexibility in your eating patterns with extra carbs to use as desired. Even on the strictest diet plan, most of these recipes should be just what the doctor ordered. Calculate how many carbs you are allowed each day and add some healthy snacks or sides to these totals. It's all up to you; just track everything.

Day 1:

Breakfast: High-Protein Yogurt Bowl: 9 net carbs - Page # 22

Lunch: Steak Salad: 1.5 net carbs - Page # 39

Dinner: Roasted Leg Of Lamb: 1 net carb - Page # 67

Cheesy Kale Casserole: 1 net carb - Page # 80

Dessert: Chocolate Muffins - Instant Pot: 5 net carbs - Page # 91

Optional Snack: Almond Milk & Avocado Smoothie: 4 net

carbs - Page # 103

Day 2:

Breakfast: Oil-Free Blueberry Streusel Scones: 3.3 net carbs - Page # 24

Lunch: Feta Cheese Salad With Balsamic Butter: 8 net carbs - Page # 36

Dinner: Roasted Chicken & Tomatoes: 5 net carbs - Page # 61

Asparagus & Tofu Mash: 8 net carbs - Page # 77

Dessert: Pumpkin Bread: 5 net carbs - Page # 96

Optional Snack: White Chocolate Fat Bombs: 0.3 net carbs - Page # 102

Day 3:

Breakfast:Bacon Hash: 9 net carbs - Page # 16

Lunch: Salad Sandwich: 4.5 net carbs - Page # 38

Dinner: Bacon & Shrimp Risotto: 5 net carbs - Page # 52

Caprese Skewers: 7 net carbs - Page # 78

Dessert: Mini Coconut Pies: 3 net carbs - Page # 93

Optional Snack: Spinach & Cucumber Smoothies: 3 net carbs - Page # 104

Day 4:

Breakfast: Omelet Wrap With Avocado & Salmon: 6 net carbs - Page # 25

Lunch: Avocado Mint Chilled Soup: 4 net carbs - Page #40

Dinner: Stuffed Chicken & Asparagus: 2 net carbs - Page #63

Cauliflower Soufflé: 5 net carbs - Page # 79

Dessert: Strawberry Thumbprint Delights: 1 net carb - Page # 99

Optional Snack: Coleslaw Stuffed Wraps: 3 net carbs - Page # 74

Day 5:

Breakfast: Blueberry Pancake Bites: 7.5 net carbs - Page # 16

Lunch: Creamy Salmon & Pasta: 3 net carbs - Page # 49

Dinner: Quick & Easy Taco Casserole: 6 net carbs - Page # 70

Edamame Kelp Noodles: 5 net carbs - Page # 82

Dessert: Streusel Scones: 3.5 net carbs - Page # 100

Optional Snack: Chocolate Muffins - Instant Pot: 5 net carbs - Page # 91

Day 6:

Breakfast: Coconut & Walnut Porridge: 6 net carbs - Page #

Lunch: Chili Delight - No-Beans: 5 net carbs - Page #43

Dinner: Cheesy Bacon Chicken: 1 net carb - Page #54

Baked Marinara Spaghetti Squash: 5 net carbs - Page # 77

Dessert: Almond Creamy & Dark Chocolate Bombs: 2 net carbs - Page # 88

Optional Snack: 5-Minute Mocha Smoothie: 4 net carbs - Page # 103

Day 7:

Breakfast: Scallion Pancakes: 5 net carbs - Page # 27

Lunch: Asian Zucchini Salad: 7 net carbs - Page # 34

Dinner: Pork Kebabs: 3.3 net carbs - Page # 64

Garlic Zucchini – Slow Cooked: 1 net carb - Page # 82

Dessert: Shamrock Shake: 5 net carbs - Page # 97

Optional Snack: Roasted Cauliflower With Blue Cheese Sauce & Bacon: 4 net carbs - Page #77

Day 8:

Breakfast: Broccoli - Eggs & Sausage With Cheese: 4 net carbs - Page # 28

Lunch: Asiago Tomato Soup: 8.75 net carbs - Page # 39

Dinner: Spicy Mexican Lettuce Wraps: 5 net carbs - Page #62

Parmesan Onion Rings: 5 net carbs - Page #84

Dessert: White Chocolate Fat Bombs: 0.3 net carbs - Page # 102

Optional Snack: Coffee & Cream: 2 net carbs - Page # 32

Day 9:

Breakfast: Brunch Brownies: 4 net carbs - Page #18

Lunch: Jar Salad: 4 net carbs - Page # 37

Dinner: Lemon Parsley Buttered Chicken- Slow Cooked: 1 net carbs - Page # 60

Mexican Cauli-Rice: 5 net carbs - Page # 83

Dessert: Strawberries With Coconut Whip: 10 net carbs - Page # 98

Optional Snack: Cheesy Bacon-Wrapped Hot Dogs: 2 net carbs - Page # 74

Day 10:

Breakfast: Cream Cheese Eggs: 3 net carbs - Page # 30

Lunch: Baked Zucchini Noodles With Feta: 5 net carbs - Page # 48

Dinner: Chicken Enchilada Bowl: 6 net carbs - Page #54

Bread Twists: 1 net carb - Page # 87

Dessert: Orange Walnut Cookies: 4 net carbs - Page # 94

Optional Snack: Almond Blackberry Chia Pudding: 1 net carb - Page # 88

Day 11:

Breakfast: Raspberry Breakfast Pudding Bowl: 6 net carbs - Page # 26

Lunch: Mexican Chicken Soup: 5 net carbs - Page # 46-47

Dinner: Bacon Burger Cabbage Stir Fry: 4.5 net carbs - Page #67

Dessert: Coconut Granola Bars: 0.9 net carbs - Page # 92

Optional Snack: Coleslaw Stuffed Wraps: 3 net carbs - Page # 74

Day 12:

Breakfast: Mushroom Omelet: 3 net carbs - Page # 31

Lunch: Marinara Zoodles: 5 net carbs - Page #49

Dinner: Stuffed Pork Tenderloin: 3 net carbs - Page # 65

Red Pepper Zoodles: 4 net carbs - Page # 85

Dessert: Frozen Blueberry Fat Bombs: 1 net carb - Page # 92

Optional Snack: Caramelized Bacon Knots: 1 net carb - Page # 73

Day 13:

Breakfast: Tomato & Cheese Frittata: 6 net carbs - Page # 31

Lunch: Cabbage Roll 'Unstuffed' Soup: 3.3 net carbs - Page #42

Dinner: Chicken Parmesan Meatballs: 3 net carbs - Page #56

Cauliflower Mac & Cheese: 7 net carbs - Page # 79

Dessert: Peanut Butter Fudge: -0- net carbs - Page # 94

Optional Snack: Caramelized Bacon Knots: 1 net carb - Page # 73

Day 14:

Breakfast: Coconut Almond Egg Wraps: 3 net carbs - Page # 29

Lunch: Broccoli & Cheese Soup: 10 net carbs - Page #41

Dinner: Nacho Skillet Steak: 6 net carbs - Page #70

Cauliflower Spinach Bowl: 7 net carbs - Page # 80

Dessert: Walnut Orange Chocolate Bombs: 2 net carbs - Page # 100

Optional Snack: Blueberry Essence: 3 net carbs - Page #

Day 15:

Breakfast: Pumpkin Pancakes: 4 net carbs - Page # 26

Lunch: Keto Salad Nicoise: 8 net carbs - Page #38

Dinner: Shrimp Alfredo: 6.5 net carbs - Page #53

Mushroom & Cauliflower Risotto: 4 net carbs - Page # 84

Dessert: Streusel Scones: 3.5 net carbs - Page # 100

Optional Snack: Philly Cheesesteak Stuffed Peppers: 9 net carbs - Page # 75

Day 16:

Breakfast: Delicious Italian Omelet: 3 net carbs - Page # 30

Lunch: Egg Drop Soup: 3 net carbs - Page #45

Dinner: Enchilada Skillet Dinner: 7 net carbs - Page #57-58

Dessert: Peanut Butter Protein Bars: 3 net carbs - Page # 95

Optional Snack: Shamrock Shake: 5 net carbs - Page # 97

Day 17:

Breakfast: Coffee Cake: 4 net carbs - Page #20

Lunch: Ginger Walnut & Hemp Seed Lettuce Wraps: 10 net carbs - Page #36

Dinner: Lemon Garlic Chicken - Instant Pot: 4 net carbs - Page # 59

Roasted Veggies: 3 net carbs - Page # 86

Dessert: Almond Blackberry Chia Pudding: 1 net carb - Page # 88

Optional Snack: Cinnamon Smoothie: 5 net carbs - Page #103

Day 18:

Breakfast: Baked Eggs In The Avocado: 3 net carbs - Page # 27

Lunch: Carrot & Beef Soup: 3 net carbs - Page # 43

Dinner: Pork-Chop Fat Bombs: 7 net carbs - Page #64

Creamy Green Cabbage: 8 net carbs - Page #82

Dessert: Peanut Butter & Chocolate Fat Bombs: 0.8 net carbs - Page # 94

Optional Snack: Blueberry Essence: 3 net carbs - Page # 103

Day 19:

Breakfast: Lemon Waffles: 2 net carbs - Page # 23

Lunch: Avocado - Corn Salad: 4.5 net carbs - Page #34

Dinner: Chicken & Yogurt - Mango Sauce: 3 net carbs - Page #57

Red Pepper Zoodles: 4 net carbs - Page # 85

Dessert: Cream Crepes: 2.5 net carbs - Page # 92

Optional Snack: Spinach & Cucumber Smoothies: 3 net carbs - Page # 104

Day 20:

Breakfast: Spinach & Ham Mini Quiche: 2 net carbs - Page # 32

Lunch: Pomodoro Soup: 6.5 net carbs - Page #47

Dinner: Chicken Parmesan Meatballs: 3 net carbs - Page #56

Edamame Kelp Noodles: 5 net carbs - Page # 82

Dessert: Chocolate Chip Cookie Dough Fat Bomb: 2 net carbs - Page # 89

Optional Snack: Bacon Wrapped Mozzarella Sticks: 1 net carb - Page #73

Day 21:

Breakfast: Choco Breakfast Waffles: 3.4 net carbs - Page # 18

Lunch: Thai-Inspired Peanut Red Curry Vegan Bowl: 10 net carbs - Page #50

Dinner: Garlic & Thyme Lamb Chops: 1 net carb - Page # 66

Baked Marinara Spaghetti Squash: 5 net carbs - Page # 77

Dessert: Strawberry Cheesecake Fat Bombs: 0.85 net carbs - Page #98

Optional Snack: Peanut Butter Protein Bars: 3 net carbs - Page # 95

Day 22:

Breakfast: Cheesy Bacon & Egg Cups: 1 net carb - Page # 29

Lunch: Crunchy Cauliflower & Pine Nut Salad: 8 net carbs - Page # 35

Dinner: Cabbage Rolls - Slow Cooked: 4 net carbs - Page # 69

Mexican Cauli-Rice: 5 net carbs - Page # 83

Dessert: Stuffed Pecan Fat Bombs: 2 net carbs - Page # 100

Optional Snack: Bacon Guacamole Fat Bombs: 1.5 net carbs - Page #72

Day 23:

Breakfast: Flaxseed Waffles: 3 net carbs - Page # 22

Lunch: Chili & Steak Explosion - No toppings: 3 net carbs - Page #44

Dinner: London Broil - Slow Cooked: 2.5 net carbs - Page # 70

Creamy Green Cabbage: 8 net carbs - Page #82

Dessert: Pumpkin Bars With Cream Cheese Frosting: 2 net carbs - Page #95

Optional Snack: 5-Minute Mocha Smoothie: 4 net carbs - Page # 103

Day 24:

Breakfast: Creamy Basil Baked Sausage: 4 net carbs - Page # 21

Lunch: Baked Zucchini Noodles With Feta: 5 net carbs - Page # 48

Dinner: Bacon Cheeseburger: 0.8 net carbs - Page #67

Garlic Zucchini – Slow Cooked: 1 net carb - Page # 82

Dessert: Chocolate Mousse: 4 net carbs - Page # 90

Optional Snack: Bulletproof Coffee: -0- net carbs - Page # 32

Day 25:

Breakfast: Lemon Waffles: 2 net carbs - Page # 22

Lunch: Creamy Chicken Soup: 2 net carbs - Page #45

Dinner: Stuffed Pork Tenderloin: 3 net carbs - Page # 65

Mushroom & Cauliflower Risotto: 4 net carbs - Page # 84

Dessert: Strawberries With Coconut Whip: 10 net carbs - Page # 98

Optional Snack: Bacon Wrapped Mozzarella Sticks: 1 net carb - Page #73

Day 26:

Breakfast: Ham Muffins: 1.5 net carbs - Page # 22

Lunch: Beef Curry - Slow-Cooked: 5 net carbs - Page #40

Dinner: Kung Pao Chicken: 4 net carbs - Page # 58

Mexican Cauli-Rice: 5 net carbs - Page # 83

Dessert: Mini Coconut Pies: 3 net carbs - Page # 93

Optional Snack: Hot Chocolate: 1 net carb - Page # 33

Day 27:

Breakfast: Brunch Brownies: 4 net carbs - Page #18

Lunch: Greens Soup: 6 net carbs - Page # 46

Dinner: Sesame Ginger Salmon: 2.5 net carbs - Page #52

Caprese Skewers: 7 net carbs - Page # 78

Dessert: Pumpkin Bread: 5 net carbs - Page # 96

Optional Snack: Bacon Guacamole Fat Bombs: 1.5 net carbs - Page #72

Day 28:

Breakfast: Cream Cheese Eggs: 3 net carbs - Page # 30

Lunch: Asian Zucchini Salad: 7 net carbs - Page # 34

Dinner: Smothered Chicken In Creamy Onion Sauce: 3 net carbs - Page # 61

Cauliflower Soufflé: 5 net carbs - Page # 79

Dessert: Strawberry Thumbprint Delights: 1 net carb - Page # 99

Optional Snack: Cinnamon Smoothie: 5 net carbs - Page #103

Day 29:

Breakfast: Broccoli - Eggs & Sausage With Cheese: 4 net carbs - Page # 28

Lunch: Creamy Salmon & Pasta: 3 net carbs - Page # 49

Dinner: London Broil - Slow Cooked: 2.5 net carbs - Page # 70

Cauliflower Spinach Bowl: 7 net carbs - Page # 80

Dessert: Coconut Granola Bars: 0.9 net carbs - Page # 92

Optional Snack: Chocolate Mousse: 4 net carbs - Page # 90

Day 30:

Breakfast: Scallion Pancakes: 5 net carbs - Page # 27

Lunch: Steak Salad: 1.5 net carbs - Page # 39

Dinner: Chicken & Green Beans: 4 net carbs - Page #55

Cauliflower Mac & Cheese: 7 net carbs - Page # 79

Dessert: Pumpkin Bars With Cream Cheese Frosting: 2 net carbs - Page #95

Optional Snack: Coffee & Cream: 2 net carbs - Page # 32

A Final Word: Tips & Tricks For Success

I hope you have enjoyed your journey through ketosis and all of the delicious meals provided in the *Keto Diet For Beginners 2019*. I hope it was informative and provided you with all of the tools you need to achieve your goals, whatever they may be. Lastly, give your diet plan a boost using intermittent fasting. It is a process you indulge in every night when you go to sleep. Let's see how it works!

Combine Fasting With Ketosis

Intermittent fasting has grown in popularity in recent years since it has the ability to endorse higher rates of nutrient absorption in the meals you eat. It has also grown in popularity because it doesn't require adherents to change radically the types of foods you are eating, when you are eating, or even drastically alter the number of calories you consume in each 24-hour time frame. In fact, the most common type of intermittent fasting is to merely eat two - somewhat more substantial meals during a day instead of the usual three. You have so many choices for the intermittent fasting process, by only using the ketogenic diet techniques.

This makes the intermittent fasting diet plan an ideal choice for those who find they have difficulty sticking to more strict diet plans, as it only requires changing one habit; the number of meals instead of many habits all at once. It's simple enough to manage successfully over a prolonged period while at the same time being efficient enough to provide the type of results that can keep motivation levels up high once the novelty of the new way of eating begins to fade.

The secret to intermittent fasting is that its accomplishment is the simple fact that the body works contrarily in a fasting status versus a fed state, which is when your body actively digests and absorbs food. This process begins some five minutes after you have finished putting food into your body, and can last anywhere from three to five hours depending on how complicated the food is for your body to digest.

While in the fed state; your body is actively producing insulin which in turn makes it harder for it to burn fat properly. The period after digestion has occurred; the insulin levels start dropping back towards normal. This process can take (in the neighborhood) from 8-12 hours which is the buffer between the fed and fasted state. Once your insulin levels return to normal, the fasted state begins which is the period where your body will process fat most effectively. Sadly, what this means is that many people never reach the point where they can burn fat most efficiently, as they rarely go eight hours, much less twelve hours from some caloric consumption.

Make A New Set Of Table Rules:

Remember to skip the highest ranks of GPS – grains, potatoes, and sugar.

Focus on veggies, fats, and proteins. Visit a restaurant that offers a healthy salad bar, seafood spreads, carving stations, and vegetable platters. You can usually find butter, olive oil, sour cream, and cheese in plentiful supply.

Use a smaller plate. Play a mind game and fill a small plate instead of a larger one. Try it, this really works.

Take your time. Enjoy your time spend with the conversation of a friend or family member. Drink your water and sip your tea or coffee. Enjoy and feel satisfied!

Make Wise Drink Decisions: The best choice is water, tea, coffee or sparkling water. Decaf coffee or herbal tea is another excellent option. If alcohol is your craving, choose dry wine, champagne, or light beer. Also, consider spirits – straight or with a bit of club soda.

Choose Dessert Wisely: If you are still hungry, try to have another cup of tea or a cheese platter. Have a portion of berries with heavy cream. What about some cream in your coffee?

These are a few more recommendations that might help:

- *Breakfast Suggestions:* Sometimes, there is nothing better than eggs if you want to play it safe. You may be off on some of the counts but after you have used some of the recipes in this book, you will know how to gauge your eating habits for the most important meal of the day.

- *Lunchtime Suggestions:* Chicken and fish are usually good choices. Many of the restaurants now offer diet-friendly menus. Select a chicken salad or a regular salad. Just be cautious of the dressing used. Try some vinaigrette or plain vinegar.

- *Dinner Suggestions:* Always choose a fresh green veggie with a lean cut of meat as your main course. Try something in the line of a hamburger minus the bun, or a tempting entrée of broccoli and steak. Tasty!

Wheat products contain an enormous amount of carbs. This will eliminate a pita or a tortilla, baked potato, or a plate of

French fries. Ask for a substitute with another side dish. Most eating establishments will be glad to accommodate your appeal, especially if they know you're on an individual diet plan.

Pay Attention To Your Body Talk: While it is essential to keep tabs on how your body is responding to intermittent fasting, it is doubly important to monitor your vitals during the preliminary phase when your body is adjusting to the new feeding times. Some discomfort is to be expected for the first three to four weeks, but anything longer or more severe should be discussed with a doctor as soon as possible.

Finally, if you found this book useful in any way, a review on Amazon is always appreciated!

Index

Chapter 3: Keto Breakfast Options

1. Bacon Hash
2. Blueberry Pancake Bites
3. Brunch Brownies
4. Choco Breakfast Waffles
5. Chocolate Muffins - Instant Pot
6. Coconut & Walnut Porridge
7. Coffee Cake
8. Creamy Basil Baked Sausage
9. Flaxseed Waffles
10. Ham Muffins
11. High-Protein Yogurt Bowl
12. Lemon Waffles
13. Oil-Free Blueberry Streusel Scones
14. Omelet Wrap With Avocado & Salmon
15. Pumpkin Pancakes
16. Raspberry Breakfast Pudding Bowl
17. Scallion Pancakes

Ultimate Eggs

1. Baked Eggs In The Avocado
2. Broccoli - Eggs & Sausage With Cheese

3. Cheesy Bacon & Egg Cups
4. Coconut Almond Egg Wraps
5. Cream Cheese Eggs
6. Delicious Italian Omelet
7. Mushroom Omelet
8. Spinach & Ham Mini Quiche
9. Tomato & Cheese Frittata

Delicious Beverages

1. Bulletproof Coffee
2. Coffee & Cream
3. Hot Chocolate

Chapter 4: Keto Lunch: Salads - Soups & Pasta

Salad Choices:

1. Asian Zucchini Salad
2. Avocado - Corn Salad
3. Crunchy Cauliflower & Pine Nut Salad
4. Feta Cheese Salad With Balsamic Butter
5. Ginger Walnut & Hemp Seed Lettuce Wraps
6. Jar Salad
7. Keto Salad Nicoise
8. Salad Sandwich

9. Steak Salad

Soup Options:

1. Asiago Tomato Soup
2. Avocado Mint Chilled Soup
3. Beef Curry - Slow-Cooked
4. Broccoli & Cheese Soup
5. Cabbage Roll 'Unstuffed' Soup
6. Carrot & Beef Soup
7. Chili Delight - No-Beans
8. Chili & Steak Explosion
9. Creamy Chicken Soup
10. Egg Drop Soup
11. Greens Soup
12. Mexican Chicken Soup
13. Pomodoro Soup

Pasta - Rice & 'Zoodle' Choices:

1. Baked Zucchini Noodles With Feta
2. Creamy Salmon & Pasta
3. Marinara Zoodles
4. Thai-Inspired Peanut Red Curry Vegan Bowl

Chapter 5: Keto Dinner Favorites: Fish & Poultry

Fish Choices:

1. Bacon & Shrimp Risotto
2. Sesame Ginger Salmon
3. Shrimp Alfredo

Poultry Choices:

1. Cheesy Bacon Chicken
2. Chicken Enchilada Bowl
3. Chicken & Green Beans
4. Chicken Parmesan Meatballs
5. Chicken & Yogurt - Mango Sauce
6. Enchilada Skillet Dinner
7. Kung Pao Chicken
8. Lemon Garlic Chicken - Instant Pot
9. Lemon Parsley Buttered Chicken- Slow Cooked
10. Roasted Chicken & Tomatoes
11. Smothered Chicken In Creamy Onion Sauce
12. Spicy Mexican Lettuce Wraps
13. Stuffed Chicken & Asparagus

Chapter 6 Keto Dinner Options: Pork & Other Meat Favorites

Pork

1. Pork-Chop Fat Bombs
2. Pork Kebabs
3. Stuffed Pork Tenderloin

Lamb Options

1. Garlic & Thyme Lamb Chops
2. Roasted Leg Of Lamb

Other Meat Favorites:

1. Bacon Burger Cabbage Stir Fry
2. Bacon Cheeseburger
3. Cabbage Rolls - Slow Cooked
4. London Broil - Slow Cooked
5. Nacho Skillet Steak
6. Quick & Easy Taco Casserole

Chapter 7: Keto Appetizers - Side Dishes & Bread Choices

Keto Appetizers

1. Bacon Guacamole Fat Bombs

2. Bacon Wrapped Mozzarella Sticks

3. Caramelized Bacon Knots

4. Cheesy Bacon-Wrapped Hot Dogs

5. Coleslaw Stuffed Wraps

6. Philly Cheesesteak Stuffed Peppers

7. Roasted Cauliflower With Blue Cheese Sauce & Bacon

Side Dishes

1. Asparagus & Tofu Mash

2. Baked Marinara Spaghetti Squash

3. Caprese Skewers

4. Cauliflower Mac & Cheese

5. Cauliflower Soufflé

6. Cauliflower Spinach Bowl

7. Cheesy Kale Casserole

8. Creamy Green Cabbage

9. Edamame Kelp Noodles

10. Garlic Zucchini – Slow Cooked

11. Mexican Cauli-Rice

12. Mushroom & Cauliflower Risotto

13. Parmesan Onion Rings

14. Red Pepper Zoodles

15. Roasted Veggies

Bread Choice

1. Bread Twists

Chapter 8: Keto Desserts & Smoothies

Desserts

1. Almond Blackberry Chia Pudding
2. Almond Creamy & Dark Chocolate Bombs
3. Chocolate Chip Cookie Dough Fat Bomb
4. Chocolate Mousse
5. Chocolate Muffins - Instant Pot
6. Coconut Granola Bars
7. Cream Crepes
8. Frozen Blueberry Fat Bombs
9. Mini Coconut Pies
10. Orange Walnut Cookies
11. Peanut Butter & Chocolate Fat Bombs
12. Peanut Butter Fudge
13. Peanut Butter Protein Bars
14. Pumpkin Bars With Cream Cheese Frosting
15. Pumpkin Bread
16. Shamrock Shake
17. Strawberries With Coconut Whip
18. Strawberry Cheesecake Fat Bombs
19. Strawberry Thumbprint Delights
20. Streusel Scones
21. Stuffed Pecan Fat Bombs

22. Walnut Orange Chocolate Bombs

23. White Chocolate Fat Bomb

Smoothies

1. Almond Milk & Avocado Smoothie

2. Blueberry Essence

3. Cinnamon Smoothie

4. 5-Minute Mocha Smoothie

5. Spinach & Cucumber Smoothie

51225075R00124

Made in the USA
Middletown, DE
01 July 2019